DOMINION SURGES

DOMINION SURGES

Prayers, Proclamations and Decrees
for Breakthrough in Your Life, Cities and Nations

RANDY DEMAIN
Kingdom Revelation Ministries, Inc.

Published by XP Publishing
A department of XP Ministries
P.O. Box 1017
Maricopa, Arizona 85139
Unites States of America
www.XPpublishing.com

ISBN: 978-1-936101-05-4

Printed in the United States of America. For Worldwide Distribution

Dominion Surge: An intense surge of spiritual power and authority that overcomes all the power of the enemy.

ACKNOWLEDGEMENTS

Thanks to all the people of Amazing Grace Bible Fellowship who have helped forge these truths and experiences in my life. Thank you to Colleen for endless help in all my writing endeavors. Thanks to my family and my wife Debbie who allowed me time to write. Most of all, Jesus, it's You who has saved and redeemed us all – without You we could do nothing.

Randy DeMain

CONTENTS

FOREWORD

I remember only too well the power surges that we experienced on the mission field in Belize, Central America, in the '80s. We frequently were visited by a "blowing of circuits" where all our computers, lights, electrical equipment, media, and appliances were shut down without warning. Sometimes these "power-outs" came as a result of lightning storms and strong winds; sometimes through trouble at the community's power source, and other times, "who knows why?" The power would often be cut off at the most unpredictable moment. Occasionally, before we could even find a flashlight, the power would return with a surge so great that it permanently damaged our computers and other equipment. Oh, yes, I am very familiar with power surges and the irreparable damage they can produce!

I was having lunch with Randy DeMain after a film shoot at our studio in Maricopa, Arizona. He passionately shared some of his revelation on dominion surges. I actually experienced a true

Holy Spirit surge of excitement in my spirit as he shared. I said, "Randy, you MUST come and share this message with our team." I then asked him if he had a book on this subject. He replied, "I am actually currently working on it." I was ecstatic and could hardly wait to get this valuable tool into my hands! This is such a powerful and timely message. It is both prophetic and apostolic.

God's "dominion surges" will put the devil out of commission for sure, and you and I get to create the surges of Christ's dominion in the earth for His glory. This is fantastic! God's dominion power surges executed through His people will truly bring alignment in the Spirit to Kingdom values, authority, and advancement. When a community experiences these dominion surges, you will truly witness the demolishing of demonic strongholds and the establishment of the Kingdom. When families experience these surges of God-power, alignment will come into entire households. When churches experience them, they will be empowered for the greater works.

Randy DeMain gives you and me powerful keys to releasing the surges. As you read his book, *Dominion Surges*, you will receive insight, infusion, and impartation. You will be blessed, empowered, and equipped. You will never be the same!

Thanks, Randy, for giving us this valuable Kingdom tool. Keep surging! Keep blowing and demolishing the devil's circuits! You rock!

Patricia King
CEO - XP Publishing

INTRODUCTION

Agreat awakening is beginning to sound across the body of Christ! An apostolic generation is coming forth, bringing fresh truth and revelation to the wonders of the Word.

Most of the truths we have built our faith upon have come forth from great exploits and supernatural experiences of the past. But, where is the power, the conquest, the glorious majesty of God in our time? We as a generation are ready to re-engage with the supernatural!

While there are a number of dynamic principles of relationship between God and man that bring forth displays of God's awesome power, few people in the body of Christ have purposed themselves to take hold of all that is accessible to us through God's dominion over all things. Yet, with the exception of faith working through love, **dominion over the works of the devil** is our greatest victory!

This truth is our rule of engagement.

The apostle Paul writes:

…having wiped out the handwriting of requirements that was against us, which was contrary to us. And He has taken it out of the way, having nailed it to the cross. Having disarmed principalities and powers, He made a public spectacle of them, triumphing over them in it (Colossians 2:14-15).

Our relationship with God is restored; our authority, power, and dominion are restored (Matthew 28:18-20). Christ has gone before us and given us the ability to overcome.

The Awakening that has come is this: We are no longer on the defense – in Christ we have overcome! Now we are maintaining the offensive to plunder the enemy and recover all.

In January of 2009 I was in my prayer closet seeking the Lord regarding this year, when He began to show me what I call the Footstool Strategy – making our enemies His footstool (see Psalm 110:1). It was then that He gave me the phrase "dominion surges," showing me out of the book of Judges what He wanted to do. He told me, "I want you to teach My people how to do dominion surges and form alliances for conquest."

Actually, dominion surges were exercised in the past by saints who believed Christ had given them all authority to extend God's kingdom and overcome. This book is simply intended to re-engage a generation with the principles and practices of those who have gone before us – people of love, power, and dominion.

A new generation of saints, just like those of old, are coming forth once again! Their faith is strong, their victory sure:

By faith the walls of Jericho fell down after they were encircled for seven days. By faith the harlot Rahab did not perish with those who did not believe, when she had received the spies with peace. And what more shall I say? For the time would fail me to tell of Gideon and Barak and Samson and Jephthah, also of David and Samuel and the prophets: who through faith subdued kingdoms, worked righteousness, obtained promises, stopped the mouths of lions, quenched the violence of fire, escaped the edge of the sword, out of weakness were made strong, became valiant in battle, turned to flight the armies of the aliens (Hebrews 11:30-34).

Dominion Surges is about mobilizing the body of Christ into an offensive posture and restoring in us a sense of dominion and power over all the power of the enemy. It's about combining the Word, worship, the prophetic, and prayer into one. *Dominion Surges* is an equipping manual to enable the rising apostolic generation to go forth and effectively expand the dominion of the King of Kings and the Lord of Lords in their personal lives and in the areas where they live.

For some, it's perhaps an awakening to spiritual truths long forgotten and unknown truth to others. This book is intended to awaken you to deeper levels of prayer, exciting prayer, that takes you someplace and engages you into the spirit realm.

I have given scriptural references to each proclamation. However, the prayers, proclamations, and decrees in this book are not exact quotes but, rather, inspired proclamations from the Word intended to bring them to a place of application and release. By giving them voice, through prayers, proclamations, and decrees, we release the Word of God upon the earth and establish His will. God is ready to watch over His Word to perform it (see Jeremiah 1:10-12).

Surge on!

Randy DeMain

PART ONE

Chapter One

THE BREAKTHROUGH GENERATION

The one who breaks open will come up before them;
they will break out, pass through the gate, and go out by it;
their king will pass before them, with the Lord at their head.
– Micah 2:13 –

A breakthrough generation is coming forth on the horizon! It is a generation of believers who will settle for nothing less than their full inheritance in Christ Jesus.

This arising generation of determined believers refuses to be denied what is theirs by covenant right and responsibility. They believe "the promises of God in Him are Yes, and in Him Amen, to the glory of God through us" (2 Corinthians 1:20). They say, "Now thanks be to God who always leads us in triumph in Christ, and through us diffuses the fragrance of His knowledge in every place" (2 Corinthians 2:14).

The promises and prophecies of Christ will be fully experienced by a generation of overcomers, a generation who will come out and be separate, who will wash their robes in righteousness. These overcoming saints are positioning themselves to live and minister out of the presence of the Lord. They are that greatly desired church Jesus is building; the church the gates of Hades will not prevail against. This church is a militant group of believers who are filled with a sense of timing and purpose. They refuse to be denied and are determined to see His purposes fulfilled in the days ahead.

The apostolic generation that is coming forth is not satisfied with the incomplete conquest experienced by those who have come before us. While we have learned great lessons from them and have benefited greatly from their faith and sacrifice, much is yet to be overcome.

INCREASE!

Every new move of God is birthed from the womb of the old. One generation gives birth to the next. Each generation brings forth a new expression of the church, the body of Christ, into their time. The mark each generation makes on history can vary greatly, as Scripture proves out. Some generations bring reformation, some degradation. My concern is what *this* generation will do.

God's design for each generation is to bring an increased presence and manifestation of His kingdom. We see this in the prophecy found in Isaiah 9:6-7 (bold emphasis mine):

> ⁶For unto us a Child is born, Unto us a Son is given;
> And the government will be upon His shoulder.
> And His name will be called
> Wonderful, Counselor, Mighty God,
> Everlasting Father, Prince of Peace.
> ⁷*Of the increase of His* government and peace

There will be no end, Upon the throne of David and over His kingdom, To order it and establish it with judgment and justice From that time forward, even forever. The zeal of the Lord of hosts will perform this.

Isaiah the prophet declares that there will be "no end" to the increase of His government (kingdom) and peace. In other words, His government and peace will always be on the increase – continually becoming greater and greater. He goes on to say that the increase of God's government will come from heaven to earth through the throne of David. What Isaiah is telling us here is that God's government will flow from heaven to earth through believers. Spiritual authority to order and establish the Kingdom of God in the earth will come through those like David who, though a king, acknowledge and serve the King of Kings.

God never intended for any generation to be static. Each generation is meant to bring forth an increased demonstration and revelation of God's kingdom. The highest spiritual place of one generation is to be the hand-off point of the next generation. This pattern can be observed from the passing on of mantles; Moses passed his mantle on to Joshua, Elijah to Elisha, David to Solomon, and Jesus to us.

Everyone on the "receiving end" would employ the impartation to overcome and occupy their inheritance from God. Throughout biblical history, we see that the single greatest factor that determined their success was faith-filled obedience to the revelation of the Lord and His commands.

In the absence of a clear hand-off, some generations have come forth without the benefit of seeing and experiencing God's power. In these generations, the people are easily given over to the "gods" of the land. Such was the case of the "post-Joshua generation."

In Judges 2:7-12 we read (bold emphasis mine):

So the people served the Lord all the days of Joshua, and all the days of the elders who outlived Joshua, who had seen all the great works of the Lord which He had done for Israel. Now Joshua the son of Nun, the servant of the Lord, died *when he was* one hundred and ten years old. And they buried him within the border of his inheritance at Timnath Heres, in the mountains of Ephraim, on the north side of Mount Gaash. When all that generation had been gathered to their fathers, **another** generation arose after them who did not know the Lord nor the work which He had done for Israel. Then the children of Israel did evil in the sight of the Lord, and served the Baals; and they forsook the Lord God of their fathers, who had brought them out of the land of Egypt; and they followed other gods from *among* the gods of the people who *were* all around them, and they bowed down to them; and they provoked the Lord to anger.

After the days of Joshua and the elders who outlived him and had also seen the great works of the Lord, another generation arose, a generation "who did not know the Lord nor the work which He had done for Israel." They did not have the benefit of the experiences of the past generations. Added to that, they were born into a time of relative blessing and prosperity in the Promised Land. Even though the enemy had not been totally driven out, times were good. This generation did not have to fight, sacrifice, or lend themselves to danger. They enjoyed blessing simply by birth.

Without having to depend on the Lord to the degree prior generations had to embrace, this generation was easily amused and given over to the seductions in the land and to the beliefs of enemy occupants.

A Wake-up Call

Would you agree with me that our present-day generation is very much like this post-Joshua generation? We do not know the Lord or His power as fully as we should. We were born into a time of relative peace and prosperity. We have been given over to the prevailing philosophies of the land – humanism, secularism, and paganism, to name a few.

However, the situation has changed drastically in recent years and now, as our world experiences increase in acts of global terrorism and economic challenges, our lives are forever being reshaped from what we have known. Furthermore, we are becoming aware of the incomplete conquest of the plans and purposes of God in our lives. These insights are leading indicators that our generation is ripe for apostolic reformation.

Our awakening has come; the time to act is upon us. The great Bible stories of the past are ready to become the testimonies of the present. A breakthrough generation must arise in this hour, with the King going forth before us. **We must turn the tide and arise with an apostolic spirit to overcome and occupy!**

A Generation of Overcomers

Recently I was on my way to a conference. As I took my seat on the airplane, I looked down to buckle my seat belt. To my surprise, I saw in my hands, in visionary form, the letters to the seven churches found in the second and third chapters of Revelation. I was very familiar with these seven letters because I had just studied and preached several expository sermons about them.

As I was looking at these letters, suddenly the first several chapters of the book of Judges overlaid them. I could see the chapters from

Judges, yet they were transparent so that I could still see the letters to the churches.

At that very moment I heard the voice of the Lord speak strongly inside me and say, "I am raising up a generation of overcomers who will overcome all as it is written in the letters. This generation will bring forth the full revelation of redemption; they will overcome the seven cycles of sin, servitude, and rule as recorded in Judges. They will bring forth full conquest; they will overcome and occupy all areas the enemies of the Lord are dwelling in."

Friend, you and I are the believers who will overcome all! We must see this as a truth that is tangible and ready to obtain. Will you join with me to overcome all to the glory of God?

In the following pages, let's connect with principles for overcoming. I invite you to review with me tried and proven principles of conquest from the Word. Then we will apply them to places of incomplete conquest in our own lives, cities, and nations. **It's time to advance again, overcome, and occupy to the glory of His name!**

Chapter Two

ALLIANCES FOR CONQUEST

In Judges 1, Joshua had died after bringing the children of Israel as far into their inheritance as he could. After his death, a new generation stood ready and eager to fully occupy their place of inheritance.

This is a spiritual parallel of our salvation. Once born again, we are translated out of the kingdom of darkness and into the Kingdom of the Son. We can taste, see, and feel our inheritance. Our salvation is sure, our victory sure, yet there are still enemies in the land. These enemies must be driven out of our soul and our land. The place our God has given us to dwell with Him must be fully occupied, no enemies of the land left in place. Incomplete conquest is unacceptable!

However, to ensure complete conquest, certain alliances need to be made. Let's see what they are!

Aaron, Hur and Moses:

The Alliance of Prayer, Praise and the Prophetic

After Moses had brought the children of Israel out of Egypt and was preparing them to enter the Promised Land, they experienced the first unprovoked attack against them by Amalek (see Exodus 17:8-16).

Amalek was determined not to allow them to enter into their inheritance. The people of Amalek were descendants of Esau, the Edomites. We remember Esau as being more interested in the immediate gratification of his flesh than in his inheritance. He actually sold his birthright for a plate of food! But as it was for him, so it is for us. Our flesh is the first resistance that arises in us and keeps us out of our inheritance. The apostle Paul makes it clear we are to come into alliance with the Holy Spirit to overcome the flesh.

> Therefore, brethren, we are debtors – not to the flesh, to live according to the flesh. For if you live according to the flesh you will die; but if by the Spirit you put to death the deeds of the body, you will live. For as many as are led by the Spirit of God, these are sons of God (Romans 8:12-14).

God is calling forth sons and brethren to join together in the Holy Spirit to overcome the flesh, the world, and the devil.

Moses sent Joshua out to fight against the Amalekites while he stood on the hill above the battle extending the rod of God over the battle array. As long as the rod was extended, victory came to the

Israelites. But when Moses became weary and let down his hands, the battle turned in favor of the Amalekites. Then Aaron and Hur came into alliance with Moses and with the Lord, each of them holding up one of Moses' hands.

This alliance represents the joining of prayer (Aaron), praise (Hur), and prophetic proclamation (Moses) to make a decree of the victory of the Lord. Aaron, who had the priestly anointing, represents prayer and intercession. Hur, whose name means "splendor," represents the splendor of God's praise. Moses, the prophetic type, prophesies the King's dominion as he extends his rod, which represents the scepter of the King of Kings.

Forming alliances using the conquest principles of prayer, praise, and prophetic proclamation enables the body of Christ to overcome today.

JUDAH AND SIMEON

THE ALLIANCE OF HIGH PRAISE AND INTERCESSORY PRAYER

Now, let's go back to Judges 1, where a new alliance for conquest was formed. With incomplete conquest at hand, a new strategy must be formulated, the people mobilized, and the borders secured.

> Now after the death of Joshua it came to pass that the children of Israel asked the Lord, saying, "Who shall be first to go up for us against the Canaanites to fight against them?" And the Lord said, "Judah shall go up. Indeed I have delivered the land into his hand." So Judah said to Simeon his brother, "Come up with me to my allotted territory, that we may fight against the Canaanites; and I will likewise go with you to your allotted territory." And Simeon went with him (Judges 1:1-3).

The Canaanites represented the embodiment of everything unholy and ungodly. They had to go – they had to be driven out. Their strongholds had to be loosed and their high places taken down. These ungodly people were a formidable enemy in the natural sense, but compared to the presence and power of God, they were nothing. Yet, how would the children of Israel bring an effective strike against the Canaanites' kings? Giants were also among them, as well as soldiers of renown. The Israelites gathered together and sought the Lord. He spoke to them with clarity and decisiveness: "Judah shall go up. Indeed I have delivered the land into his hand."

God gave them prophetic revelation of His strategy that would overcome kings, giants, and the best warriors when he instructed, "Judah shall go up." Judah, as the first to go out, was a principle throughout all of Israel's occupation efforts. This principle remains as true for us today as it was in that day.

However, it is verse 3 that gives us the fuller tactic for today. It is our example of alliances for conquest. Judah said to Simeon, his brother, "Come up with me to my allotted territory that we may fight against the Canaanites; and I will likewise go with you to your allotted territory."

Here is the significance of this alliance; Judah means "praise" – but not just any kind of praise. It means to excitedly and aggressively raise up a decree of God's Word in thanksgiving, blessing and worship: "God, You are awesome! God, You cause me to overcome! I bless You today because You make me more than a conqueror!" There is an interesting prophecy over Judah in Genesis 49:8: "Judah... your hand shall be on the neck of your enemies." When we're praising God, our hand is on the neck of our enemies!

Simeon, on the other hand, means "heard," as it relates to prayer and intercession. When we join together in praise and intercessory prayer to sound forth the proclamations of the Lord, we activate the full force of power and authority given to men. **When we combine high praise, prayer, and proclamation to utter forth the decrees of the Lord, God's enemies are dislodged and our full occupation secured.**

In recent times, there has been a mobilizing of the body of Christ to prayer, prophecy and praise that enthrones the Lord. Each of these virtues alone has come forth with great effectiveness. But, up until now, we have seldom implemented them together because we have lacked understanding of the great power and effect they have when combined. Look at the words of Psalm 149:3-9:

> [3] Let them praise His name with the dance;
> Let them sing praises to Him with the timbrel and harp.
>
> [4] For the Lord takes pleasure in His people;
> He will beautify the humble with salvation.
>
> [5] Let the saints be joyful in glory;
> Let them sing aloud on their beds.
>
> [6] *Let* the high praises of God *be* in their mouth,
> And a two-edged sword in their hand,
>
> [7] To execute vengeance on the nations,
> And punishments on the peoples;
>
> [8] To bind their kings with chains,
> And their nobles with fetters of iron;
>
> [9] To execute on them the written judgment –
> This honor have all His saints.
> Praise the Lord!

God is ready to execute the written judgment upon His enemies who defy His name and who stand against His purposes. He is ready to bruise the head of the devil (Genesis 3:15), to bind earthly and spiritual kings and princes with chains and with fetters of iron as we play our instruments, sing and dance before the Lord.

As we lift up our voices in prophetic declaration, God reaffirms us as His children.

> "I will declare the decree: The Lord has said to Me, 'You are My Son, Today I have begotten You. Ask of Me, and I will give You the nations for Your inheritance, and the ends of the earth for Your possession' " (Psalm 2:7-8).

It's time for the Levites to come forth and restore praise and worship as a weapon. The key of David (spiritual praise and worship) must come forth again, bringing unity to sound, words, declarations, and decrees, thus releasing the kingly anointing upon the people to arise and overcome.

The key must be inserted into the locks of the enemy's strongholds through militant praise and declaration. The enemy's gates must be overtaken and then replaced with gates of praise and salvation. We need to see *ourselves* as the spiritual gates the Lord of Glory comes through. He will give us victory over our enemies as we praise His name:

> [7] Lift up your heads, O you gates!
> And be lifted up, you everlasting doors!
> And the King of glory shall come in.
>
> [8] Who *is* this King of glory?
> The Lord strong and mighty, The Lord mighty in battle.

⁹ Lift up your heads, O you gates! Lift up, you everlasting doors!
And the King of glory shall come in.

¹⁰ Who is this King of glory? The Lord of hosts,
He *is* the King of glory. *Selah* (Psalm 24:7-10).

It's time for brothers to "go up" together, following Judah and Simeon's example. Churches and ministers need to lay aside their agendas and join together, combining their unique strengths for the greater cause.

The kingly anointing is ready to emerge from hiding to a place of prominence. Kings rule by their words; the decree of the Kings of Kings must come forth out of our mouths into the atmosphere in order to conquer our enemies.

Many today, like the 400 men who joined David, are weary of the man-pleasing spirit that has left them distressed, in debt, and discontented. They recognize the kingly anointing and are forming alliances with those who are coming forth to overcome. They are lending their skills, talents and abilities to the emerging King.

WE NEED BOTH PRAISE AND WORSHIP

The apostolic spirit that carries the government of God must begin to raise up and release apostolic worship leaders who bring forth prophetic sounds and decrees. The last several decades have majored in worship at the expense of praise. The effect is obvious, as we sit quietly worshiping our King while the enemy rolls in and takes over.

It has been said regarding praise and worship:

- Praise enjoys God. Worship esteems Him.
- Praise acclaims Him. Worship beholds Him.

31

- Praise lifts. Worship bows.

- Praise lauds. Worship loves.

- Praise celebrates. Worship humbly reveres.

- Praise addresses God. Worship waits on God.

- Praise dances. Worship removes shoes for Holy Ground.

- Praise exults God for what He has done. Worship extols Him for who He is.

- Praise lifts us to heavenly places. Worship lifts God to His rightful place.

- Praise enters into warfare. Worship is adoration.

- Praise warfare sends a message to satanic forces. Worship sends incense to the throne.

- Praise says, "Praise the Lord." Worship demonstrates, "He is the Lord."

- Praise is grateful for heirship to the throne. Worship lays crowns at His feet.

We need both praise and worship. Praise breaks loose strongholds, bringing you into the land. Worship is what you do after conquest.

ENCOUNTERS WITH ANGELS

A few years ago I had two revelatory encounters with messenger angels. During the first one I was instructed to listen to the voice of the seventh messenger, the voice recorded in the letter to the church of Laodicea in chapter three of Revelation. A week later, I was awakened out of sleep and found myself in the presence of an angel of the Lord who said, "It's 444 time. Listen to the voice of the seventh angel."

The seventh angel brings forth the revelation of the seven

thunders of God, among many other things. The overcomers are instructed to eat the little book and prophesy again about many peoples, nations, tongues, and kings. I understood that the "444" was a reference to Psalm 44:4: "You are my King, O God; Command victories for Jacob." These victories are already prepared, victories awaiting those who will prophesy the decree of the Lord. **Let's arise and prophesy the victory of our God, then to move forward and occupy our inheritance!**

Leviticus 26:7-12 says:

[7] You will chase your enemies, and they shall fall by the sword before you.

[8] Five of you shall chase a hundred, and a hundred of you shall put ten thousand to flight; your enemies shall fall by the sword before you.

[9] For I will look on you favorably and make you fruitful, multiply you and confirm My covenant with you.

[10] You shall eat the old harvest, and clear out the old because of the new.

[11] I will set My tabernacle among you, and My soul shall not abhor you.

[12] I will walk among you and be your God, and you shall be My people.

It is time for churches, ministries, cities, states, and regions to form "alliances for conquest" and join forces together to overcome, take ground, gain harvest, and occupy enemy territory – occupy *our* inheritance!

Chapter Three

WHEN YOU HEAR THE SOUND

*And it shall be, when you hear the sound of marching in the tops
of the mulberry trees, then you shall advance quickly. For then the
Lord will go out before you to strike the camp of the Philistines."*

– 2 Samuel 5:24 –

The apostolic anointing establishes strong praise. A militant
praise creates a prophetic atmosphere, which in turn causes
a progression of supernatural events to take place. Let's look
at that progression.

First, the voice of the Lord comes forth out of this prophetic
atmosphere, announcing His intentions and thus posturing His
people to plunder the enemies' camp. This sound from heaven
captivates the people, drawing them into heavenly places. From this
place, they begin to act and speak experientially in response to the
presence of His glory. Clothed with radiant joy, they shout unto
God with voices of triumph and praise that invade the earth. Next,
all of heaven is activated in response to the people's proclamations

and decrees that are invading the earth with truth. The Lord of Hosts responds, exercising His spiritual dominance and authority over the areas of resistance that His people are encountering. Breakthrough is achieved and the people arrive at their desired place. This is the essence of a successful campaign!

The purpose of the throne of David and the essence of David's tabernacle is to provide a place of habitation and rule for the Lord on the earth. Its purpose is to see "Your Kingdom come, Your will be done on earth as it is in heaven."

Now, let's revisit together a couple of biblical accounts that teach us principles regarding the sounds that activate heaven.

Sounds that Were Deadly Weapons

Jehoshaphat was one of Israel's greatest reformers. In his generation, he took down the high places of false worship and restored the ministry of the priests and Levites. After a time of successful reform, the people of Moab, Amman, and others joined together to battle against Jehoshaphat. It is amazing how quickly resistance comes once you set yourself to overcome and establish righteousness! Moab was known as the "land of loose living." The people of Amman were characterized by their cruelty, pride and idolatry.

The report came to Jehoshaphat of the mounting insurgence. He set himself and his people to a time of prayer and fasting throughout Judah. People from all the cities of Judah (praise) gathered together to ask help from the Lord.

The prayer of Jehoshaphat follows:

Then Jehoshaphat stood in the assembly of Judah and Jerusalem, in the house of the Lord, before the new court, and said: "O Lord God of our fathers, *are* You not God in heaven, and do You *not* rule over all the kingdoms of the nations, and in Your hand *is there not* power and might, so that no one is able to withstand You? Are You not our God, *who* drove out the inhabitants of this land before Your people Israel, and gave it to the descendants of Abraham Your friend forever? And they dwell in it, and have built You a sanctuary in it for Your name, saying, 'If disaster comes upon us—sword, judgment, pestilence, or famine—we will stand before this temple and in Your presence (for Your name *is* in this temple), and cry out to You in our affliction, and You will hear and save' " (2 Chronicles 20:5-9).

The Lord hears from heaven and replies:

And he said, "Listen, all you of Judah and you inhabitants of Jerusalem, and you, King Jehoshaphat! Thus says the Lord to you: 'Do not be afraid nor dismayed because of this great multitude, for the battle *is* not yours, but God's. Tomorrow go down against them. They will surely come up by the Ascent of Ziz, and you will find them at the end of the brook before the Wilderness of Jeruel. You will not *need* to fight in this *battle*. Position yourselves, stand still and see the salvation of the Lord, who is with you, O Judah and Jerusalem!' Do not fear or be dismayed; tomorrow go out against them, for the Lord *is* with you" (2 Chronicles 20:15-17).

Many wonder how the simplicity of prayer, praise, and proclamation can win battles, overturn principalities and powers, and release the blessings of the Lord. The answer is just as profoundly simplistic (bold emphasis mine):

Do not be afraid nor dismayed because of this great multitude, **for the battle is not yours, but God's** (verse 15b).

You will not need to fight in this battle. Position yourselves, stand still and see the salvation of **the Lord, who is with you** (verse 17).

The response of the king, the Levites, and Kohathites (praise and worship leaders) to God's Word was outstanding. They stood up to praise the Lord God of Israel with voices loud and high. The next morning they went out at the Word of the Lord, appointing those who were to sing to the Lord and praise Him for the beauty of His holiness. As they went out before the armies, they sang, "Praise the Lord, for His mercy endures forever." An amazing victory unfolded:

> Now when they began to sing and to praise, the Lord set ambushes against the people of Ammon, Moab, and Mount Seir, who had come against Judah; and they were defeated.
>
> When Jehoshaphat and his people came to take away their spoil, they found among them an abundance of valuables on the dead bodies, and precious jewelry, which they stripped off for themselves, more than they could carry away; and they were three days gathering the spoil because there was so much (2 Chronicles 20:22, 25).

The joining of the kingly, priestly and prophetic anointing to go out and engage the enemy is a proven principle to overcome the enemies of the Lord!

PREPARATION BEFORE THE SOUND

When David became fully king of both Judah (2 Samuel 2) and Israel (2 Samuel 5), he set out to destroy all the Lord's enemies from the land once and for all.

The Philistines were one of David's last enemies. When they heard that David had been anointed king of Israel, they promptly set themselves against him to deny him his occupation and kingly rule. The Philistines are symbolic of the uncircumcised flesh – that which needs to be removed to fully receive all covenant blessings. This includes pride that's unwilling to submit to God and pride that believes one has greater ability than another.

Before we continue, let's backtrack a little. When the Israelites first recognized David as their king, David was still living in Hebron. Hebron is the place of commitment, because David's heart was set on nothing less than complete conquest and occupation. Here at Hebron, he is anointed for the third time. His first anointing had happened years before, after Saul disobeyed God. David was then anointed to replace Saul (1 Samuel 16:13). His second anointing had happened later on, after military victories resulted in the death of Saul. Judah then anointed him as king (2 Samuel 2:4). In 2 Samuel 5:3 we find the third anointing when all the tribes assembled together, reunited to anoint him king over all of them.

Take note of the progression that occurs to bring forth the kingly anointing to wage war and overcome.

The first anointing could be seen as an outcome of Saul's failure, as he desired to please men more than God. For David, it was the anointing of the flesh, the sanctifying of the body of flesh unto the Lord.

The second anointing can be seen as the sanctifying of the soul, removing from the soul the tares of unfruitful chaff to allow the spirit to come into proper place.

The third anointing is the crowning anointing that releases kingly rule. It is the anointing upon the spirit to bring forth the fullness of God.

Because of these three anointings, now David was fully prepared to take on the Philistines! When he was faced with issues of the flesh and soul, he overcame because his flesh and soul were sanctified unto the Lord. The Philistines pushed over and over again the insecurities and weakness of the flesh and soul, but David was now fully moving in the Spirit, in the fullness of the kingly anointing.

The Philistines deployed themselves in the Valley of Rephaim. This valley is known as the valley of fallen spirits, the corrupted angelic stronghold of giants – disembodied demonic spirits awaiting a host to manifest in. It was as if they were drawing David into the most powerful place of demonic strongholds possible. This was apparently a last ditch effort to overcome the king lest he overcome them. The Bible records:

> So David inquired of the Lord, saying, "Shall I go up against the Philistines? Will You deliver them into my hand?" And the Lord said to David, "Go up, for I will doubtless deliver the Philistines into your hand." So David went to Baal Perazim, and David defeated them there; and he said, "The Lord has broken through my enemies before me, like a breakthrough of water." Therefore he called the name of that place Baal Perazim (2 Samuel 5:19-20).

David had come to a place of spiritual purity and purpose in the Lord; the Philistines (the flesh) could no longer overpower him. David went out by the power of the Lord and overcame and defeated the Philistines. The presence and power of the Lord flooded the battlefield. So great was the victory, David named the place Baal Perazim, which translates, "Master of breakthrough."

THE "SURROUND SOUND" THAT OVERCAME THE ENEMY

The proud Philistines rallied on and attempted one more time to overcome David. This time the Lord gave David a new strategy – "surround sound"! It's almost comical that the Lord told David to circle around behind them and then come upon them in the front of the mulberry trees. It was as if the Lord was saying, "If the Philistines refuse to acknowledge Me and be circumcised, I will use David to overcome them and give Me their foreskins." So He instructed David, "Circle around them, David, circumcise them in front of the balm trees, where healing balm is available. David, when you hear the sound, the 'surround sound' of marching in the top of the trees, advance quickly. I have sent my war angels to bind and crush the demonic spirits just below them, as you strike the Philistines."

What was the outcome? "So David did what the Lord commanded, and he struck down the Philistines all the way from Gibeon to Gezer" (2 Samuel 5:25 NLT).

The kingly apostolic anointing is creating an atmosphere of sound – heavenly sounds and earthly sounds. It is the "surround sound" that will overcome all our enemies, seen and unseen, so we may restore the presence of the Lord to our cities and our people.

The warring angels are ready to come forth on our behalf. They are dispatched as we give voice to the Word of the Lord, as we declare, decree, sing and shout His Word.

¹⁹ The Lord has established His throne in heaven,
And His kingdom rules over all.

²⁰ Bless the Lord, you His angels,
Who excel in strength, who do His word,
Heeding the voice of His word.

[21] Bless the Lord, all you His hosts,
You ministers of His, who do His pleasure.

[22] Bless the Lord, all His works,
In all places of His dominion.
Bless the Lord, O my soul!

(Psalm 103:19-22 bold emphasis mine)

When you and I give faith-filled sound to the Word of the Lord, it is like God's voice to the angels. Therefore, being assigned to fulfill the commanded Word of the Lord, they go forth, out from our prophetic prayer, praise, and proclamation. When we hear them marching above us, it's our signal to "go up quickly," for the Lord has given the victory into our hands!

CHAPTER FOUR

PROPHETIC PRESSURE PRINCIPLE

All of creation is embedded with DNA that responds to the voice of the Lord. This is an important principle to understand when persevering to see a prophetic word fulfilled. In many cases, all we need to do is apply sufficient prophetic pressure to the words that have been spoken in order to see them come to pass.

Elijah is an excellent example of one who applied the principle of "prophetic pressure." Elijah stood before the Lord regarding the activities of Ahab and Jezebel. He was incensed over the carnality of King Ahab and overwhelmed by Jezebel's false prophets who were leading a godly nation into Baal worship. The Lord then placed a prophetic mantle upon Elijah of great authority and power. So great was this mantle that even the elements of the earth were subject to his voice.

And Elijah the Tishbite, of the inhabitants of Gilead, said to Ahab, "As the Lord God of Israel lives, before whom I stand, there shall not be dew nor rain these years, except at my word (1 Kings 17:1).

God put the entire destiny of a nation in the mouth of one man: *"There shall not be dew nor rain these years, except at my word."*

God was utilizing Elijah to confront and expose the false Baal worship. Baal was worshipped as the "god of weather." To prove that He, not Baal, was the true Lord of the weather, He had Elijah stop not only the rain but even the dew, so no one could say Baal was still in charge. At the word of Elijah, there was no rain or dew for three and a half years!

Then Elijah had the showdown at Mount Carmel with the hundreds of prophets that were under Jezabel's wing. There Elijah proved once again that God is the Most High God over all. Right after, in an interesting turn of events, Elijah began to call forth the rain.

Up to this point, whatever Elijah spoke would come to pass the first time he called it out. He commanded the rain and dew to stop. It immediately did. He spoke over the widow of Zarephath's flour and oil, resulting in supernatural multiplication. After the untimely death of the widow's son, Elijah was able to restore him back to life. None of his words had fallen to the ground, until now. Scripture records that this time, Elijah had to call forth the rain seven times before it responded!

I asked the Lord why it took just one time for the rain and dew to stop, yet seven times for it to begin. The answer was both shocking and delightful. The Lord revealed to me that the moment Elijah spoke to Ahab and released the word regarding the dew and rain, the demonic spirits empowering Baal set themselves to nullify the word. It was too late to try and bring forth the dew and rain, so the strategy was to keep it from raining when the time came. This would cause Elijah to be considered a false prophet, and Baal still large and in charge.

The demonic forces built layer after layer of resistance in the realm of the spirit to keep Elijah's words from activating the dormant dew and rain. Therefore, Elijah had to continue to put pressure on the prophetic word until it broke through. "Rain!" he called out. One layer penetrated. "Rain!" The second layer broken through. "Rain!" came the command through deep intercession, until finally on the seventh power-packed decree, breakthrough! The DNA in creation quickly rallied to fulfill the prophetic word as if it were the Lord's very own voice. The cloud formed and the rain came. Jezebel's false prophets were silenced and the true prophetic voice restored in the land.

Many of us have had prophetic words spoken over us that remain unfulfilled. Perhaps what we need to do to see our words fulfilled is to re-engage them, speak them out and keep pressure on them. Of course, God's timing is a factor we must also take into consideration.

Paul exhorted Timothy: "This charge I commit to you, son Timothy, according to the prophecies previously made concerning you, that by them you may wage the good warfare, having faith and a good conscience, which some having rejected, concerning the faith have suffered shipwreck" (1 Timothy 1:18-19).

Prophecies should be seen as weapons which we use to wage good warfare. We must be diligent to steward the prophecies spoken over us, as well as the prophecies yet to be fulfilled in Scripture, by applying prophetic pressure on them with the spoken word.

"BEHIND THE SCENES"

Now take a look with me at the story of Deborah and Barak in Judges 4 and 5. Here we can get a clear picture of what takes place when "prophetic pressure" is placed on a word that has been given from God.

The children of Israel had suffered twenty years of harsh oppression by Jabin, king of Canaan, when Deborah the prophetess received the word of the Lord.

> Then she sent and called for Barak the son of Abinoam from Kedesh in Naphtali, and said to him, "Has not the Lord God of Israel commanded, 'Go and deploy *troops* at Mount Tabor; take with you ten thousand men of the sons of Naphtali and of the sons of Zebulun; and against you I will deploy Sisera, the commander of Jabin's army, with his chariots and his multitude at the River Kishon; and I will deliver him into your hand'?" And Barak said to her, "If you will go with me, then I will go; but if you will not go with me, I will not go!" So she said, "I will surely go with you; nevertheless there will be no glory for you in the journey you are taking, for the Lord will sell Sisera into the hand of a woman." Then Deborah arose and went with Barak to Kedesh (Judges 4:6-9).

Deborah had received a word from the Lord to release her people from captivity. However, Barak wasn't as excited about the word as she was. He was a military commander of troops without weapons, troops Deborah was calling forth against an army of 900 chariots of iron!

She was spiritual and prophetic. He was carnal and a realist. He did his best to talk Deborah out of going forward with the word of the Lord. Deborah refused to not act on the word; she knew she must steward the word, release it, and put pressure on it. She was finally able to get Barak's cooperation and set out for conquest.

The battle ended up being an easy victory for Barak. God caused such a heavy rainstorm that the iron chariots became stuck in the mud, making Jabin's army easy prey. We don't find this out until we read Deborah and Barak's victory song in the following chapter. There we can clearly see what happened behind the scenes, which reveals the power of the prophetic word when it's released and when pressure is put on it through faith-filled responses.

> 4"Lord, when You went out from Seir,
> When You marched from the field of Edom,
> The earth trembled and the heavens poured,
> The clouds also poured water;
>
> 5The mountains gushed before the Lord,
> This Sinai, before the Lord God of Israel.
>
> 6In the days of Shamgar, son of Anath,
> In the days of Jael, The highways were deserted,
> And the travelers walked along the byways.
>
> 7Village life ceased, it ceased in Israel,
> Until I, Deborah, arose, Arose a mother in Israel.
>
> 8They chose new gods; Then there was war in the gates;
> Not a shield or spear was seen among forty thousand in Israel."
> (Judges 5:4-8)

Verse 4 rolls back the curtain and allows us to see how a stewarded prophetic word is fulfilled:

"Lord when You went out from Seir, when You marched from the field of Edom, the earth trembled and the heavens poured, the clouds also poured water."

Wow, did you catch that? I thought it was ten thousand men of the sons of Naphtali and of the sons of Zebulun who brought the victory. But no! The song of Deborah reveals it was the Lord who went out, embodied in the troops that day. It was the Lord making sure His word, the word He had given through the prophetess Deborah, would be fulfilled!

How awesome is this? **When you and I speak out the Word of the Lord and then move towards its fulfillment, prophetic pressure overcomes the dark realm of resistance and the Lord of Hosts brings forth our victory!**

If that isn't awesome enough, **the prophetic word spoken and acted upon also activates the angelic realm to battle the unseen forces that resist us.** Let's read some more.

> [18] "Zebulun is a people who jeopardized their lives to the point of death, Naphtali also, on the heights of the battlefield.
>
> [19] The kings came and fought, Then the kings of Canaan fought in Taanach, by the waters of Megiddo;
> They took no spoils of silver.
>
> [20] They fought from the heavens;
> The stars from their courses fought against Sisera."
> (Judges 5:18-20)

"They" fought from the heavens against Sisera, the commander of Jabin's army. Who are the "they" in verse 20? The stars (the lighted princes) refer to the angels – they fought the powers of darkness over their appointed geographical courses (area), their spiritual grids of travel.

THE POWER OF PROPHETIC SONGS AND DECREES

The value of the prophetic word is immeasurable when spoken out or brought forward through prophetic song or decree. When alliances for conquest are in place, the prophetic word is released and acted upon. The prophetic pressure to bring forth its fulfillment is released against the powers of darkness.

In 1998, my wife and I started Amazing Grace Bible Fellowship in Redmond, Oregon. After we grew from six to about twenty people, we began to employ strong prayer and decrees during our services. Within a short period of time, we moved out of our rented hotel room to our first building. We continued to engage the realm of the Spirit with passionate praise, proclamation, and decrees. Within a year, we went from 80 to 200, from one service to two. We moved again to a larger facility where the church continues to expand in influence.

During the past several years, we have witnessed our city experience a spiritual and physical makeover. Many churches in our area have doubled, some even tripled. Dark havens of illicit activities have been shut down. Our city has prospered greatly. While there is much left to do, much has been accomplished through our dominion surges.

We have also done dominion surges in some churches in other cities. As a result, they, too, have experienced increase after years of no or minimal growth. So when people ask me for an effective church growth strategy, my answer is "praise and proclamation!"

Get your words out, get your alliances in place, apply prophetic pressure and get ready for breakthrough!

ERECTING A SIEGE MOUND

A powerful strategy for the attacking forces to overtake well-entrenched strongholds and fortified cities was to erect a siege mound against them (2 Kings 24:10-11). A siege mound shuts down all flow of traffic or trade to the stronghold; additionally, it could provide a means of entrance over or through walls and gates. Once the supply of basic essentials to support life and replacement inventory for defense is cut off, it is only a matter a time until the ability to sustain the stronghold is depleted.

An effective siege demoralizes the defenders, reduces their strength, and cuts off reinforcements. Once this is accomplished, death and surrender are the only alternatives for those in the stronghold.

I have utilized this principle against enemy strongholds large and small with great effectiveness. We have set ourselves against immoral and illegal activities in our city and region, assaulting the realm of the Spirit with prayers, proclamations, and decrees. Some strongholds came down quickly. Others took more time, but the outcome has been the same: Victory is assured as we continue the siege!

I have often employed this principle in praying for people who are experiencing chronic or terminal illness. I keep steady pressure against the illness with prayer and proclamations of truth with authority and power. We cut off the voice and strength of the illness until it surrenders and they recover.

As a person is being trained to use dominion surges, he or she is required to practice pressing in with sustained effort over some strongholds until they are weakened sufficiently to a place of surrender.

Isaiah chapter twenty-three records the prophetic decree of the fall of Tyre and Sidon, two evil strongholds that embraced revelry and wickedness at any cost. The Lord purposed to set a siege against them that would destroy them in the manner they had destroyed others. This siege resulted in a shift. The material and financial wealth formerly in the hands of the wicked was transferred to the people of the Lord (Isaiah 23:12-18).

Our prayers, proclamations, and decrees become a siege mound against enemy strongholds. If we will arise and build our siege mound, wickedness can be cut off and overcome in our midst. It's time to assemble our camps. It's time to plunge our battering rams of holy decrees into the gates of our enemies! It's time to plunder the enemy of captivated souls, misused wealth, and resources!

The second part of this book is filled with powerful decrees, prayers, and proclamations that will drive out enemy strongholds, allowing our occupation. Let our praises be weapons in the hand of the Lord. Let our intercession become nation-changing and our proclamations become like fruitful vines.

CHAPTER FIVE

PREPARATION FOR PRAISE PURSUITS

D o you realize that, from the very beginning of the creation of man, a covenant was established that imparted an apostolic spirit to mankind? I'm referring to the Edenic covenant between God, Adam, and Eve.

Then God said, "Let Us make man in Our image, according to Our likeness; let them have dominion over the fish of the sea, over the birds of the air, and over the cattle, over all the earth and over every creeping thing that creeps on the earth." So God created man in His *own* image; in the image of God He created him; male and female He created them. Then God blessed them, and God said to them, "Be fruitful and multiply; fill the earth and subdue it; have **dominion** over the fish of the sea, over the birds of the air, and over every living thing that moves on the earth" (Genesis 1:26-28).

"Be fruitful and multiply; fill the earth and subdue it; have dominion" summarizes the basic components of the covenant. Most of us are well aware of this covenant, which in fact is reaffirmed throughout the entire Old Testament. What may be surprising to some is that this very same covenant is actually brought forward to us in the New Testament! The language is a little different, but the components remain the same:

> Jesus came and spoke to them, saying, "All authority has been given to Me in heaven and on earth. Go therefore and make disciples of all the nations, baptizing them in the name of the Father and of the Son and of the Holy Spirit, teaching them to observe all things that I have commanded you; and lo, I am with you always, even to the end of the age." Amen (Matthew 28:18-20).

In this command, Jesus has restored man's eternal created purpose on earth. He has restored us as sons and daughters in right standing with God the Father.

- We have unrestricted access into God's presence to obtain mercy and grace.
- We have the unrestricted flow of covenant blessings.
- We have restored sonship, authority, and power.
- We have unrestricted ability to :
  1. Be fruitful and multiply.
  2. Fill the earth and subdue it.
  3. Have dominion over all God's creation.

If we overlay the Great Commission (Matthew 28:18-20) upon the Edenic covenant, it looks like this:

- Go therefore and make disciples of all the nations.
  (Be fruitful and multiply.)

- Teach them to observe all things that I have commanded you.
  (Fill the earth and subdue it.)

- Baptize them in the name of the Father and of the Son and of the Holy Spirit.
  (Have dominion over all the earth.)

- I am with you always, even to the end of the age.
  (My dominion mandate will not end until He has put all enemies under His feet.)

This dominion mandate extends over all that Christ Jesus overcame, including sin, sickness, disease, and even death.

WE ARE MEANT TO BE KINGS!

God's original plan was for man to share His authority and rule, not serve Him like a servant. This is why Jesus is described as "King of Kings and Lord of Lords" (Revelation 19:16b), not "King of servants." God is interested in kings like Himself. He wanted sons who would not only be led by the King, but also exercise authority as a king on the earth. God gave man His image and likeness, and then placed him in His presence. God's greatest desire is that we act like Him and live with Him.

After Adam's sin, we lost dominion and His presence. Man on several occasions tried to restore this relationship. The first attempt came from Cain and Abel, when they offered sacrifices unto God. Instead, it had a tragic outcome, failing to restore relationship and the dominion mandate.

Man's next attempt came from Noah after the flood wiped wickedness from the earth. After the flood, Noah built an altar to the Lord and brought Him a pleasing sacrifice. This reconnect resulted in a partial reinstatement of the mandate but lacked the dominion aspect, "Be fruitful and increase in number and fill the earth." God did not command Noah to subdue the earth, have dominion and rule over it. Why? Through sin, man lost his right to dominion. This is a picture of believers today who restore worship only, but fail to pursue the dominion mandate.

Next in line is Abraham, to whom God promised land and people. Then came David, who rose up to restore God's presence, power, and dominion through the Tabernacle of David and eventually the throne of David. He operated in the kingly and priestly anointings that we are meant to operate in, and came into the dominion God intends us to have!

THE DOMINION MANDATE IS ON!

When we are fully aware of both our rights and responsibilities for dominion within the covenant we have with Him, as well as our position as kings, we are fully prepared to take on our praise pursuits. The dominion mandate is on!

It's time to set ourselves apart to the Lord, like Joshua instructed the people to do – the new generation ready for conquest:

So it was, when all the kings of the Amorites who were on the west side of the Jordan, and all the kings of the Canaanites who were by the sea, heard that the Lord had dried up the waters of the Jordan from before the children of Israel until we had crossed over, that their heart melted; and there was no spirit in them any longer because of the children of Israel.

At that time the Lord said to Joshua, "Make flint knives for yourself, and circumcise the sons of Israel again the second time." So Joshua made flint knives for himself, and circumcised the sons of Israel at the hill of the foreskins. And this *is* the reason why Joshua circumcised them: All the people who came out of Egypt *who were* males, all the men of war, had died in the wilderness on the way, after they had come out of Egypt. For all the people who came out had been circumcised, but all the people born in the wilderness, on the way as they came out of Egypt, had not been circumcised. For the children of Israel walked forty years in the wilderness, till all the people *who were* men of war, who came out of Egypt, were consumed, because they did not obey the voice of the Lord – to whom the Lord swore that He would not show them the land which the Lord had sworn to their fathers that He would give us, "a land flowing with milk and honey." Then Joshua circumcised their sons *whom* He raised up in their place; for they were uncircumcised, because they had not been circumcised on the way" (Joshua 5:1-7).

It's time to arise and shine, and prepare for occupation. It's time to see a restoration of what has been stolen by the enemy and to take new ground. David was attacked at Ziklag by the Amalekites. They burned the city with fire and took captive the women, children, and possessions. Even though the people spoke of stoning him, he moved a distance away for a while to encourage himself in the Lord.

So David inquired of the Lord, saying, "Shall I pursue this troop? Shall I overtake them?" And He answered him, "Pursue, for you shall surely overtake *them* and without fail recover *all*" (1 Samuel 30:8).

It's time to make fresh alliances for conquest, for if we pursue, we will recover all. The prophet Isaiah tells of the Lord's desire to restore His people to a place of dominion.

But this *is* a people robbed and plundered;
All of them are snared in holes,
And they are hidden in prison houses;
They are for prey, and no one delivers;
For plunder, and no one says, "Restore!" (Isaiah 42:22)

If it is in your heart to see the things taken from us restored, if you are weary of incomplete conquest, then it's time for dominion surges: Purposefully gathering together to pursue and recover all, to lift up our voice of praise and proclaim, "Restore."

You and I were made for this; we are seated with Christ in heavenly places (Ephesians 2:6-7)! We are not trying to overcome; we have overcome! **It's time to stir ourselves and see ourselves as God does; in Him we are overcomers, more than conquerors! What are you waiting for?**

CHAPTER SIX

SETTING YOUR GPS

(Glory Positioning System)

To have an effective dominion surge, it is important to plug in some crucial data: Where do you intend to go? How are you going to get there? What do you expect after you arrive? The Bible is filled with great examples of dominion surges. The Old Testament is replete with intentions and descriptions of battles to take lands, cities, and peoples. Ask yourself: What is the scope of your battle? Is it your neighborhood, city, region, or state? What is your expected geographical impact?

A BIBLICAL DEFINITION

To be clear about the terminology of a *dominion surge*, a look at biblical definitions is enlightening:

Dominion: (Strong's Concordance, #7287)

To rule, have dominion, dominate, tread down, subjugate

Surge: (Strong's Concordance, #1607)

To shake, quake, to be shaken up, convulsed

Gesenius's Lexicon:

To push, to thrust. Syr. To push with a horn.

Dominion is related to military, civil or spiritual rule by dominion.

"Surge" is likened to the movement of waters, particularly overwhelming flood waters, or the excessive power of a wave to move and overcome all in its path. "Surge" is like the power of an earthquake to loose foundations, structures, and strongholds. "Surge is like the push or thrust of an invading army into enemy territory at the sound of the horn."

When you combine "dominion" and "surge," the purpose and dynamic is clear: **It is a tactical thrust forward into enemy territory to tread down, overcome, occupy, and rule.**

JESUS ORCHESTRATED A NUMBER OF DOMINION SURGES

Jesus began by fasting in the desert to prove His dominion over the world, the flesh, and the devil. **The focus of this dominion surge was righteousness and holiness.**

His next dominion surge was to infiltrate the land and people in His local area with the Kingdom of heaven:

From that time Jesus began to preach and to say, "Repent for the kingdom of heaven is at hand" (Matthew 4:17).

One important step was to gather His disciples and train them for dominion surges:

> Then He said to them, "Follow Me, and I will make you fishers of men." They immediately left their nets and followed Him. Going on from there, He saw two other brothers, James the son of Zebedee, and John his brother, in the boat with Zebedee their father, mending their nets. He called them, and immediately they left the boat and their father, and followed Him.
>
> And Jesus went about all Galilee, teaching in their synagogues, preaching the gospel of the kingdom, and healing all kinds of sickness and all kinds of disease among the people. Then His fame went throughout all Syria; and they brought to Him all sick people who were afflicted with various diseases and torments, and those who were demon-possessed, epileptics, and paralytics; and He healed them. Great multitudes followed Him – from Galilee, and from Decapolis, Jerusalem, Judea, and beyond the Jordan (Matthew 4:19-25).

Jesus did dominion surges for healing, deliverance, and restorative miracles. The result was great multitudes came to Him and followed Him. He did surges for harvest (Matthew 9:35-38) and other Kingdom causes as well.

It's Time for Positioning

We can do a dominion surge in the same way, or tailor it uniquely to our calling. We can launch a surge with a single focus or create a more comprehensive surge like Jesus did:

- **Prophetic Proclamation:** "The Kingdom of heaven is at hand."

- **Prophetic Assimilation:** Gathering disciples

- **Prophetic Demonstration:** Jesus went about…healing

- **Kingdom Occupation:** "And when He had called His twelve disciples to Him, He gave them power over unclean spirits, to cast them out, and to heal all kinds of sickness and all kinds of disease" (Matthew 10:1).

- **Kingdom Proliferation:** "After these things the Lord appointed seventy others also, and sent them two by two before His face into every city and place where He Himself was about to go" (Luke 10:1).

All dominion surges should begin with a gathering of individuals who will bring forth a prophetic decree of the word and works of the Kingdom of God. These proclamations, prayers, and decrees should charge and impregnate the atmosphere with authority and power. Then an ensuing action based upon the focus of the surge must be taken. If the focus is harvest (John 4:35-38), send out the harvesters. If it is healing, go and pray for the sick. The more clear and specific you are, the greater the intensity of the surge.

Another key factor for a successful dominion surge is to understand the nature of our enemy and engage the right weapons. Ephesians chapter six makes our focus clear:

For we do not wrestle against flesh and blood, but against principalities, against powers, against the rulers of the darkness of this age, against spiritual hosts of wickedness in the heavenly places (Ephesians 6:12).

Verses 13-18 of chapter six go on to exhort us of the necessity of putting on the proper armor before we engage in battle. We are to put on Christ Jesus, fill our mouths with the testimony of Jesus, plead the blood, and go willing to give the surge our all.

Our ability to overcome and conquer is assured. Our victory is complete.

> For though we walk in the flesh, we do not war according to the flesh. For the weapons of our warfare *are* not carnal but mighty in God for pulling down strongholds, casting down arguments and every high thing that exalts itself against the knowledge of God, bringing every thought into captivity to the obedience of Christ, and being ready to punish all disobedience when your obedience is fulfilled (2 Corinthians 10:3-6).

> And they overcame him by the blood of the lamb and the word of their testimony, and they did not love their life to the death (Revelation 12:11).

Setting your GPS (glory positioning system) should also include prayers, proclamations, and decrees regarding the uniqueness of the geography where the surge will take place. People live in varying geographical locations with climates, terrain, and cultures. The Scriptures are filled with insightful information regarding the location and manifestation of certain spiritual strongholds unique to the geography. Some good research is beneficial in aiming your spiritual assault for ultimate effectiveness. Local information and insight can turn your shotgun into a laser beam, as one identifies strongholds in the area.

In regards to the terrain, the Bible speaks of mountains, valleys, islands, hills, and plains. Deserts are often mentioned as places of significant spiritual activity, both good and bad. Animalistic spirits and other mediums host spirits of wickedness in all types of terrain that can be identified and liberated.

63

In the following pages, I have listed prayers, proclamations, and decrees that you can customize to your surge setting. Take the time to review the lists, fill your quiver and sharpen your sword with decrees for your area. Use them as you see fit.

PREPARATION FOR DOMINION SURGES

As you prepare, take hold of the following scriptural truths and principles:

Life and death are in the power of the tongue (Proverbs 18:21). The words we speak are spirit and life (John 6:63). While we can be snared by the words of our mouths, rightly spoken words carry force and power (Job 6:25).

We have been given the keys to the Kingdom (Matthew 16:19). The keys are the ability to bind and to loose. To bind means to tie, wind, fetter, restrict, hold back. To loose means to untie, unlock, liberate, release, free, and forgive.

When we speak forth the words of the Lord as sons and daughters of the Most High God (John 1:1-14), our words carry the authority and power of heaven, the presence and power of the Holy Spirit (Romans 8:12-17).

Our words bind the strongman that we may plunder (surge) his house (Matthew 12:29).

Our words untie, unwind, and liberate the purposed blessings of the Lord that the devil came to steal, kill, and destroy. Loosing the word restores our flow of abundance (John 10:10).

"For the Lord will plead their cause, and plunder the soul of those who plunder them" (Proverbs 22:23).

"No one can enter a strong man's house and plunder his goods, unless he first binds the strong man. And then he will plunder his house" (Mark 3:27).

PUTTING YOUR DOMINION SURGES INTO ACTION

A dominion surge can take on a variety of shapes and expressions. Since I have a background in music and the word, I see dominion surges through those scriptural lenses. I'm after the restoration of the house (tabernacle) of David as mentioned in Acts 15:16-17. Taking this into account, my dominion surges would revolve around gathering together a group of like-minded people (10 or 100,000) who can establish an environment in the Spirit for the release of prayers, proclamations, and decrees.

We would have decided in advance the focal point of the surge. For example, it could be healing, harvest, holiness, or perhaps a general blast to dislodge the enemy in the realm of the Spirit, allowing us to move into a greater degree of occupation.

Since music, praise, and the prophetic are an integral aspect of the surge, I would gather musicians and singers who can flow in the Spirit with songs of the Spirit and songs of understanding. Once the atmosphere and environment are properly prepared, we (the musicians, singers, attendees, and myself) would begin to pray, making proclamations and decrees to the sounds and rhythms of music. I would begin with the appropriate lists in this book, and then allow the Spirit to lead. It's important to declare blessings after the curses have been overcome.

A dominion surge can be for one day or up to seven days until all decrees are fully released. **Once the decrees are released, the people are now ready to go forth to plunder the strongman's house.**

[1] The Lord said to my Lord, "Sit at My right hand,
Till I make Your enemies Your footstool."

[2] The Lord shall send the rod of Your strength out of Zion.
Rule in the midst of Your enemies!

[3] **Your people shall be volunteers**
In the day of Your power;
In the beauties of holiness, from the womb of the morning,
You have the dew of Your youth.

[4] The Lord has sworn
And will not relent,
"You are a priest forever
According to the order of Melchizedek."

[5] The Lord is at Your right hand;
He shall execute kings in the day of His wrath.

[6] He shall judge among the nations,
He shall fill the places with dead bodies,
He shall execute the heads of many countries.

[7] He shall drink of the brook by the wayside;
Therefore He shall lift up the head.

(Psalm 110:1-7, bold emphasis mine)

And what *is* the exceeding greatness of His power toward us who believe, according to the working of His mighty power which He worked in Christ when He raised Him from the dead and seated *Him* at His right hand in the heavenly *places,* far above all principality and power and might and dominion, and every name that is named, not only in this age but also in that which is to come. And He put all *things* under His feet, and gave Him *to be* head over all *things* to the church, which is His body, the fullness of Him who fills all in all (Ephesians 1:19-23).

"Knowing that Christ, having been raised from the dead, dies no more. Death no longer has dominion over Him" (Romans 6:9).

"For sin shall not have dominion over you, for you are not under law but under grace" (Romans 6:14).

When we go forth in a surge of dominion, it has an incredible effect on the enemies of the Lord.

"A voice of crying shall be from Horonaim" (Jeremiah 48:3).

"They will drink and stagger and go mad because of the sword that I will send among them" (Jeremiah 25:16 NASB).

Rise up mighty ones, a dominion surge is in the wind!

"Then Caleb quieted the people before Moses, and said, 'Let us go up at once and take possession, for we are well able to overcome it' " (Numbers 13:30).

Gather the people, determine the focus of your surge, prepare the decrees and begin. You can do it!

PART TWO

Many of the prayers, proclamations, and decrees in the following chapters are not exact quotes but, rather, inspired proclamations from the Word intended to bring them to a place of application and release.

CHAPTER SEVEN

IDENTIFYING YOUR TERRAIN

MOUNTAINS AND HILLS

"These *are* the statutes and judgments which you shall be careful to observe in the land which the Lord God of your fathers is giving you to possess, all the days that you live on the earth. You shall utterly destroy all the places where the nations which you shall dispossess served their gods, on the high mountains and on the hills and under every green tree. And you shall destroy their altars, break their *sacred* pillars, and burn their wooden images with fire; you shall cut down the carved images of their gods and destroy their names from that place." – Deuteronomy 12:1-3.

* Let us become like a new threshing sledge with sharp teeth to thresh the wickedness from the mountains. Let wickedness in the high places be brought low, let the hills become like chaff. – Isaiah 41:15.

- Listen, O mountains in this place; hear the word of the Lord God! For the word of the Lord says to the mountains, to the hills, to the ravines, and to the valleys: "Indeed I, even I, will bring a sword against you, and I will destroy your high places."
  – Ezekiel 6:3

- Let every mountain now hear the voice of the Lord and be removed. – Micah 6:2

- I contend with you, O mountains of this land, and command you to hear my voice. – Micah 6:1

- I now command every mountain set against me to be removed and cast into the sea. – Mark 11:23

- Make waste every evil mountain in my life, O Lord.
  – Isaiah 42:15

- Bring the mountain of Esau (works of the flesh) to waste.
  – Malachi 1:3

- O God, You are against every destroying mountain.
  – Jeremiah 51:25

- Put forth Your mighty hand, O Lord, and overturn the mountains by the roots. – Job 28:9

- Let the mountains now tremble at the presence of God.
  – Habakkuk 3:10

- Let the mountains melt at Your presence; let them become like wax. – Psalm 97:5

- I prophesy to you, O mountains in my land; I command you to hear the word of the Lord and be removed. – Ezekiel 36:4

- No mountain shall stop my ministry unto the Lord; they shall become like a plain before me with shouts of grace! Grace! – Zechariah 4:7

- I call forth to the mountains in this place and decree the decree of the Lord: "The mountains will bring peace to the people, and the little hills, by righteousness." Come forth, peace; come forth, righteousness. – Psalm 72:3

- Listen, people of this land, "For you shall go out with joy, and be led out with peace; The mountains and the hills shall break forth into singing before you, and all the trees of the field shall clap their hands." – Isaiah 55:12

- "Now it shall come to pass in the latter days that the mountain of the Lord's house shall be established on the top of the mountains, and it shall be exalted above the hills; and all the nations shall flow to it." – Isaiah 2:2

- "And it will come to pass in that day that the mountains shall drip with new wine." – Joel 3:18

- Let unity come among the brethren, let unity release the precious anointing oil, let the oil come forth like the dew of Mount Hermon, descending upon the mountains of Zion. Let now the commanded blessings of the Lord come forth! – Psalm 133:1-3

ISLANDS

Islands are mountains surrounded by water. They are places of salvation from the storm, places of both exile and miracles. They are fruitful places of international trade. An island is what you make it. Paul healed the sick there; John received great revelation on Patmos. Position yourself and your island in the Word and release God's glory!

- Lord, we raise up pure hands to deliver the people of the islands. – Job 22:30 KJV

- Let the false prophets of the islands be blinded and silenced by the decree of the Lord, let Your mighty power deliver them in Your salvation. – Acts 13:6-12

- Lord, send forth Your fire upon Your enemies in the coastlands, then they will know You are the Lord. – Ezekiel 39:6

- Lord, release dreams, visions, revelation and translations to those separated unto You on the islands. – Revelation 1:9

- Lord, let Your islands be for salvation, refreshing and blessing. – Acts 27:16, 27, 28

- Let healing miracles come forth and manifest on the islands. – Acts 28:8,9

- Let new songs come forth to the Lord, and His praise from the ends of the earth, you who go down to the sea, and all that is in it, you coastlands and you inhabitants of them. – Isaiah 42:10

- Let now Your righteousness draw near us. Send forth Your salvation. Stretch out Your hand, O Lord, to judge the peoples. "The coastlands will wait upon Me, and on My arm they will trust." – Isaiah 51:5

HIGH PLACES

- Right now I break all agreements with hell over my life, my dwelling place, my ministry. – Isaiah 28:18

- I fully renounce and break free from all ungodly oaths made by my ancestors and family members to idols, demons, false religions and unholy organizations, in the mighty name of Jesus. – Matthew 5:33

- I annul and break loose from all unholy covenants made with idols and demonic entities by my bloodline, in Jesus' name. – Exodus 23:32

- I command all unholy, unclean spirits to no longer follow me or influence me or others through me. Depart from my presence forever! – Matthew 8:16,17

- Let every false ministry in high places be removed. – 1 Kings 12:31

- Let now all false worship be removed, be silenced, in the high places. – 2 Chronicles 28:25

- Let the former moves of God that have become idols (Nehushtan) be removed from their high places and destroyed. – 2 Kings 18:4

- Let now the religious spirits be cast down from the high places. – 2 Kings 23:8

- Let the places of witchcraft be destroyed in Jesus' name in every place I walk and speak. – 2 Chronicles 28:4

- Lord, let now the high places be purged through Your anointed ones. – 2 Chronicles 34:3-7

- Let the high places built by my ancestors be destroyed.
  – 2 Kings 18:4

- I bind the high places once destroyed from being rebuilt.
  – 2 Chronicles 33:3

- Let all high places in my area established by ungodly rulers be now broken down and removed in Jesus' name. – 2 Kings 19:5

- Let now every satanic altar in high places be taken down, destroyed, and removed in Jesus' mighty name.
  – 2 Chronicles 14:2-5

- Let now righteous men come forth with the wisdom of the Lord. Let them come forth and be seated in the high governmental places of my city, state, and nation. – Proverbs 9:3

- Lord, in Jesus' name, open rivers in the high places.
  – Isaiah 41:18

- Let Your people now ride on the high places of the earth, let them eat the increase of the fields, let them suck honey out of the rock and oil out of the flinty rock. – Deuteronomy 32:12-13

- Lord, let Your voice, the voice of My Beloved, sound forth over us, come to us leaping upon the mountains, skipping upon the hills. – Song of Solomon 2:8

PLAINS

Plains as experienced in Scripture are places of preparation, provision, and positioning for breakthrough. God spoke to His people on the plains of Moab and Jericho, preparing them for what was to come. Moses and the priest spoke with the people on the plains of Moab by the Jordan River. Plains have been places of encampment, markers of freedom, places of fruitfulness and agricultural bounty.

• Lord, let the vision and revelation of our inheritance be seen from this place. – Numbers 21:1

• Lord, let Your priests speak in the plains, let Your people arise and be counted as those who will serve the Lord. – Numbers 26:3,4

• Let now the enemies of the Lord be plundered from the plains, let the booty and spoil come into the hands of Your people. – Numbers 31:12

• Let Your words and Your commands, O Lord, regarding family, inheritance, and marriage, be upheld as a standard and witness of the Lord from the plains. – Numbers 36

• Let not the people of the plains resist the new ways, the new leadership of the Lord; rather let the Joshuas arise, let us cross over and occupy all that is ours! – Deuteronomy 34:1-2

• Lord, let the people of the plains place their faith in the blood of Jesus. – Joshua 5:10

• Let the people of the Lord wait upon the Lord until His word comes forth. – 2 Samuel 15:28

• Let wells be dug in this place, wells of the Lord to release His blessings, His living water. – 2 Chronicles 26:10

VALLEYS AND LOWLANDS

- Lord, fight against the spirits of the valley withstanding the purposes of God. Let my enemies be avenged in the valley. – Joshua 10:12-14

- I smite the Edomite spirit in this valley in Jesus' name. – 2 Kings 14:7

- I smite the Midianite spirit of poverty in my valley with the sword of the Lord. – Judges 6:33

- I smite the spirit of Amalek in my valley in Jesus' name. – 1 Samuel 15:3-5

- Let the enemies' chariots be broken and destroy those who war against the valley and the lowlands. – Judges 1:19

- Let the heart of David once again overcome the giants in my valley. I rebuke and cut off the spirit of Goliath that would challenge me. – 1 Samuel 17:1-4

- Let now the giants of the valley be decapitated. Let their own swords be used against them. – 1 Samuel 17:41-51

- Let the Philistines be cut off in the Valley of Rephaim, let not them stir up the unclean spirits of that place. – 2 Samuel 5:18

- I break the seductive spirit of Delilah over the strongman of the land operating in this valley. – Judges 16:4

- Lord, let every valley in my life be exalted. – Luke 3:5

- Let every low place be filled in that restricts the way of the Lord to my life, my valley. – Isaiah 40

- Let water come forth and flow in my valley. – Joel 3:18

- Let my valley be blessed in Jesus' name – 2 Chronicles 20:26

- Lord, give us vineyards here, let our valley become like the Valley of Achor, a door of hope. – Hosea 2:15

- Let all those who deny that You are the Lord of the valleys be removed from this place. – 1 Kings 20:28

- Let our valley be covered with herds of livestock and fields of grain, let us shout for joy and sing unto the Lord. – Psalm 65:13

DESERTS

The desert has its uniqueness and beauty like none other. When water is supplied to the dry and arid places, life springs forth in abundance. The desert is a place of trial and temptation, a place to reckon with the frailties of humanity. The desert is the place many have come forth from with great revelation and power. The desert is a well-known place of angelic activity, evangelism, and salvation.

- Let the unclean spirits of the wilderness now bow and lick the dust of the desert. – Psalm 72:9

- Let Your voice, O Lord, shake the desert and let the saints shout "Glory!"

- Let Your goodness and Your abundance drop upon my desert places. – Psalm 65:11-12

- I command the Pharaoh spirit to let the people go three days' journey into the desert to bring the sacrifice of praise unto the Lord. – Exodus 5:3

- Lord, establish Your mountain in our desert that we may experience You as Moses did. – Exodus 3:1

- Lord, find us here in the desert land, encircle us, instruct us and keep us as the apple of Your eye. – Deuteronomy 32:9-10

- Let the highway of holiness be established here; let the lame leap like a deer, and the tongue of the mute sing. Let waters burst forth in the wilderness and streams in the desert. – Isaiah 35:6

- Let the voice of one crying in the wilderness be heard, let the way of the Lord be prepared; let a straight way be established in the desert, a highway for our God! – Isaiah 40:3

- Let the new things spring forth and be made known from the desert; let a revelatory road, a flowing river of revelation, burst forth. – Isaiah 43:19

- Let Your comfort, O Lord, come to the people of the desert; let gladness and joy be found here, heard here. – Isaiah 51:3

- Let the people of the Lord come through trial and temptation with great power. Let them come forth releasing the Kingdom of heaven. – Luke 4:1,14

- Lord, let now the angels who gather come forth; let them direct our evangelism efforts and direction. – Acts 8:26

- In Jesus' name, I take authority over the animalistic spirits who dwell in this place. I bind your activity and rebuke your presence from your unclean hosts. Leave this place in Jesus' name! – Isaiah 13:21,22; 34:10-15

- Lord, now open rivers in high places and fountains in the midst of the valleys. We call forth pools in the wilderness and springs in the dry places. – Isaiah 41:18

CHAPTER EIGHT

WARFARE PRAYERS AND DECREES

- Lord, as I now enter into warfare against spiritual forces of darkness with understanding of the advancement of Your Kingdom, I pray You will cover my head in the day of battle (Psalm 140:7). Cover me with the shadow of Your hand (Isaiah 51:16), cover me with Your feathers (Psalm 91:4), be my defense and refuge (Psalm 59:16). Lord, You are my shield and my protection (Psalm 51:2), I cover my doorpost and my possession with the blood of Jesus (Exodus 12:13), I release the voice of the blood against demons, against evil spirits who would seek to harm, accuse or condemn me — I declare you shall not prevail. I bind your activity and schemes from prospering against me, my family, and ministry. The Lord rebuke you, Satan (Zechariah 3:2, Hebrews 12:24, Matthew 16:18).

- You, O Lord, have given me the necks of my enemies; I will destroy them in Jesus' name. — Psalm 18:40

- I will beat my enemies as fine as dust before the wind; I cast them out like dirt in the street. – Psalm 18:42

- Let my enemies be wounded to the point they are unable to rise, let them fall under my feet. – Psalm 18:38

- I will now arise, thresh, and beat my enemies into pieces. – Micah 4:13

- I bind and rebuke every demon who now attempts to block my way. In Jesus' name, yield entrance to my path. – Matthew 8:28

- I overcome every unclean spirit because greater is He that is in me than he that is in the world. – 1 John 4:4

- Let every hidden snare for my feet be exposed. – Jeremiah 18:22

- I am released unharmed from every snare and scheme of the devil. – 2 Timothy 2:26

- Lord, give me strength to overcome and bring forth my destiny. – Isaiah 66:9

- Teach my hands to war and my fingers to fight. – Psalm 144:1

- Let all the enemies that make war with the Lamb be taken out and destroyed. – Revelation 17:14

- I tread upon serpents and scorpions and over all the power of the enemy, and nothing by any means shall harm me. – Luke 10:19

- I loose myself from the spirit of error in Jesus' name; I loose and rebuke the operation of a wrong spirit in my life. – 1 John 4:6; Luke 9:55

- I expose and cast down in Jesus' name false apostolic, prophetic, and teaching ministries in my area. Let them be gagged and silenced. – 2 Corinthians 11:13; Matthew 7:15; 2 Peter 2:11

- Let every false vision or prophetic word released into my life be exposed; I fully reject them in Jesus' name. – Jeremiah 14:14

- I renounce all earthly, sensual, and demonic wisdom. – James 3:15

- I bind the spirit of Absalom from operating in my life and the life of the church, that would steal our hearts and allegiance from God's ordained leadership. – 2 Samuel 15:6

- Lord, cleanse me from my secret faults and presumptuous sins – Psalm 19:12

- Deliver me out of the hand of wicked and unreasonable people. – 2 Thessalonians 3:2

- Lead me in a clear path because of my enemies. – Psalm 27:11

- I renounce ungodly anger, and I give no place to the devil. – Ephesians 4:27

- I loose myself from every bond of the devil in Jesus' name. – Luke 13:16

- Lord, remove Satan's seat from my region. – Revelation 2:13

- In Jesus' name, let every synagogue of Satan be exposed and destroyed in my city. – Revelation 3:9

- Let the confidence of the enemy be rooted out. – Job 18:14

- Lord, let every root of bitterness be uprooted out of my life. – Hebrews 12:15

- Let the counsel of the wicked be spoiled. – Job 12:17

- "Destroy, O Lord, and divide their tongues." – Psalm 55:9

- I loose confusion against every demonic conspiracy against my life. I bind the spirit of Sanballat and Tobiah in the name of Jesus. – Nehemiah 6:1-6

- I break in two and cast down every demonic confederacy formed against me in Jesus' name. Make the ruling spirits of these confederacies come to the same end as Oreb, Zeeb, Zebah and Zalmunna. – Psalm 83:5-13

- Persecute all demonic confederacies formed against me with Your tempest and Your storms; let them become confounded and troubled, let them be put to shame; loose confusion on them and let them attack each other. – Psalm 83:15-17; 2 Chronicles 20:23

- I am delivered from destruction that wasted at noonday. – Psalm 91:6

- I rebuke, in Jesus' name, all destruction from my gates. – Psalm 24:7

BREACHES IN THE WALL

- I pray for a hedge of protection around my mind, body, soul and spirit. Lord, hedge my possessions, loved ones, finances, and family, in Jesus' name. – Hosea 2:6

- I close up every breach in my life that gives Satan and his unclean spirits access in Jesus' name. – Ecclesiastes 10:8

- Bind up all my breaches, O Lord. – Isaiah 30:26

- Father, I ask in Jesus' name every broken hedge in my life to be repaired. – Ecclesiastes 10:8

- I am a rebuilder and restorer of the breach. – Isaiah 58:12

- Let my walls be salvation and my gates praise. – Isaiah 60:18

DISMANTLING WITCHCRAFT AND CAULDRONS

- My enemy will not eat my flesh, break my bones or put me in his cauldron. – Micah 3:3

- The Lord will protect me from every pot of calamity. – Jeremiah 1:13-14

- I am delivered from the boiling pot in Jesus' name. – Ezekiel 24:1-5

- I rebuke and destroy every wicked cauldron in Jesus' name. Lord, visit every witch and warlock in my region; let them repent and be saved. – Ezekiel 11:11-12; Acts 19:19

- Lord, destroy witchcraft in our midst. – Micah 5:12

- Lord, let me not operate in rebellion, which opens the door to the spirit and sin of witchcraft. I renounce rebellion out of my heart and declare I have a submissive heart unto the Lord and His anointed. – 1 Samuel 15:23

- I renounce and loose from myself all enhancements pronounced by witches against me. I rebuke familiar spirits sent forth by wizards from my life. Be forever gone in Jesus' name. – 2 Chronicles 33:6

- Expose those among us who practice divination, sorcery, and witchcraft, and let them be removed. – Deuteronomy 18:10

- Let all those enslaved by witchcraft be loosed in my area in Jesus' name! – Nahum 3:4

YOKES AND BURDENS

- Let every yoke of bondage be destroyed in Jesus' name.
  – Galatians 5:1-3

- Let every unequal yoke be broken. – 2 Corinthians 6:14

- Lord, let the anointing now come forth, and break every enemy yoke from my neck, let every yoke be destroyed. – Isaiah 10:27

- I remove all false expectations, burdens, religion, and weights placed on me by leaders, people, and churches.
  – 1 Thessalonians 2:6

- Jesus, I take now Your yoke upon me, for Your yoke is easy, Your burden light. – Matthew 11:28-30

- Now in Jesus' name, I break the yoke of the enemies' burden, and break the staff and rod of oppression as in the day of Midian.
  – Isaiah 9:4

- Let now every burdensome stone be removed from me in Jesus' name. I bless Jerusalem, the city of the Lord. – Zechariah 12:3

TERRORISM

- In the name of Jesus, I declare the word of the Lord: "Violence shall no longer be heard in (my) land." I bind up acts of terrorism, devastation, and fear within my borders. – Isaiah 60:18

- I bind up and rebuke all terrorism plots against my land and people; Lord, expose the plans of the terrorists.

- Deliver me from violent and bloodthirsty men. Preserve us from violent men who plan evil in their hearts. I bind their tongues and lips from speaking. – Psalm 140:1

- Let the gathering of violent men be cut off and exposed; let the mob be disbursed. – Psalm 86:14

- I loose acts of violence out of the hands of the wicked and bind their evil paths and thoughts against me. – Isaiah 59:6-8

- I will not be afraid of terror by night. – Psalm 91:5

CHAPTER NINE

RELEASING THE WEAPONS OF THE LORD

THE BLOOD

- Lord, let Your wonders come forth in the heavens and in the earth: blood and fire and pillars of smoke against Your enemies. – Joel 2:30-31

- Lord, because of the blood of Your covenant, set the prisoners free from the waterless pit. – Zechariah 9:11

- Lord, forgive me and release me from the guilt of the shed blood of the prophets; release and forgive Your people through the blood of Jesus. – Matthew 23:30-35

- Jesus, I eat Your body and drink the cup of Your blood now activating the new covenant in my life. I believe in Your name, I depend upon Your blood for the remission of sins. Thank You for freedom! – Matthew 28:26-29; John 6:35

- Lord, Your flesh is food indeed, and Your blood drink indeed. I eat Your flesh and drink Your blood that I might abide in You and You abide in me. – John 6:55-56

- I am purchased by the blood of Christ Jesus; I am His and no other's. I take heed to myself and those the Lord has given me to oversee to keep them in Christ Jesus. – Acts 20:28

- I am justified by the blood of Jesus and saved from the wrath to come. – Romans 5:9

- I drink the cup of blessing, the righteousness of God, and declare my freedom from the curse of the law. – 1 Corinthians 10:16

- I have been brought near by the blood of Jesus; I have redemption in His blood, the forgiveness of sins. I have been reconciled unto God and have peace. Death is now destroyed, the devil is destroyed and I have eternal life in the presence of God. – Ephesians 1:7; 2:13; Colossians 1:14, 20

- I have no spot, my conscience is clean, and the accuser of the brethren, the devil, has no hold on me. I'm free from dead works to now serve the living God. – Hebrews 9:14

- I am made perfect by the blood of the everlasting covenant. – Hebrews 13:20-21

- I enter the holiest by the blood of Jesus. I come to obtain mercy and find grace to bring forth to my generation – grace to live, to overcome, and to walk in liberating power over all the power of the enemy. – Hebrews 4:16; 10:19

- I release the voice of the blood against every evil spirit that accuses, condemns, and oppresses me. Let the blood bring forth freedom and release better things. – Hebrews 12:24

- I wash my robes in the blood of Jesus and come out from among those that are defiled by the flesh. – Revelation 7:14

- I plead the power of the blood of Jesus over all that's been given unto me. Let now the power of the blood to redeem, protect, provide, and restore be fully activated over me. – Exodus 12:13

- I overcome Satan and all his works by the blood of the Lamb and by the word of my testimony, and I do not love my life over my willingness to give it for the cause of Christ.
  – Revelation 12:11

THE FIRE

- O God, cause Your glorious voice to be heard, release the lightning of Your indignation down Your arm against Your enemies in this place. Let your devouring flame of fire come forth with scattering, tempest, and hailstones and beat down Your enemy. – Isaiah 30:30-31

- Let all flesh see the release of Your fire. – Ezekiel 20:48

- Let demonic schemes and weapons be exposed and cast out by Your fire. – Acts 28:3

- Let the writing and works of witchcraft be overcome by Your great power; let the books and equipment be burned by fire.
  – Acts 19:19

- Let burning coals fall on evil lips; let the words and works of darkness be cast into the fire, into deep pits, that they may not rise again. – Psalm 140:10

- Let fire and brimstone rain down upon the spirits of lust and perversion; let the harboring cities deliver the righteous and destroy their wicked. – Genesis 19:24

- Release Your hot thunderbolts against the enemy. – Psalm 78:48

- Lord, come and rebuke Your enemies with flames of holy fire. – Isaiah 66:15

- Let Your light be a fire, and Your Holy One a flame to burn the thorns and briers, the plantings of the enemy, out of my life, my city, and region in a day. – Isaiah 10:17

- Purify my life with Your holy fire. – Malachi 3:1-2

- Let Your fire be released in Zion, Your church. – Isaiah 31:9

- Purge my lips with coals from Your altar. – Isaiah 6:5-6

- Let Your fire cover and protect me; reveal Your glory and power to me. – Exodus 14:24

- Baptize me in the Holy Spirit and fire. – Luke 3:16

- Let me preach Your word with fire; let fire be in my heart, my hands, my belly, and my mouth to heal the sick and cast out devils. – Jeremiah 20:9; 23:29

- I quench every fiery dart of the enemy with the shield of faith. – Ephesians 6:16

- I quench every fire of the enemy in the sanctuary in Jesus' name. – Psalm 74:7

- I will not be burned by any fire of the enemy. – Isaiah 43:2

- I bind the enemy from burning up my harvest. – 2 Samuel 14:30

- O Lord, You are the God who answers by fire; release Your fire on my obedience, my sacrifice, until the people's hearts are restored to you. – 1 Kings 18:24,36-39

THE ARM OF THE LORD

- Your right hand and Your holy arm give me victory. – Psalm 98:1

- No one has an arm like You, O Lord, filled with overcoming power and might. – Job 40:9

- Lord, "You have a mighty arm; strong is Your hand, and high is Your right hand. Righteousness and justice are the foundation of Your throne; mercy and truth go before Your face." – Psalm 89:13-14

- Stretch out Your arm and deliver me from all bondage. – Exodus 6:6

- Let great dread and fear come upon my enemies by the great power of Your arm until I pass over. – Exodus 15:6

- Favor me, let Your right arm bring me into my possession. – Psalm 44:3

- Let Your hand establish me, let Your arm strengthen me. – Psalm 89:10

- Let the power in Your hands be fully released upon my life. – Hebrews 3:4

- Let power and might be released from Your hand. – 1 Chronicles 29:12

- I trust in Your arm for my salvation. – Isaiah 51:5

- Lord, let us experience in our day the mighty strength of Your arm to heal and deliver. Stretch out Your arm and give us boldness. – Acts 4:29-30

95

- "Awake, awake, put on strength, O arm of the Lord! Awake as in the ancient days, in the generations of old. Are you not the arm that cut Rahab apart, and wounded the serpent?" Awake for us now in our generation! – Isaiah 51:9

- Make bare Your holy arm in the sight of all nations; let all flesh see Your salvation. – Isaiah 52:10

THUNDER AND LIGHTNING

- "The adversaries of the Lord shall be broken in pieces; from heaven He will thunder against them. The Lord will judge the ends of the earth. He will give strength to His king, and exalt the horn of His anointed." Lord, release Your thunders as You have spoken. – 1 Samuel 2:10

- Send forth thunders, O Lord, against our enemies to confuse them, that we might overcome them. – 1 Samuel 7:10

- Lord, we call to You in our troubles so that You will do again as You have done before: answer us and deliver us in the secret place of thunder. – Psalm 81:7

- Send forth Your rebuke, O Lord, the voice of Your thunder, and scatter our enemies.

- Let sons of thunder arise again in our day and time; let them come forth in great power, signs, and wonders. – Mark 3:17

- Let the revelations of the heavens, the seven thunders, come forth to us. – Revelation 6:1; 10:2-4; 14:2

- Lord, let us see Satan fall like lightning. – Luke 10:18

- Lord, let us witness the thunders, the lightning, and the flashes of God, the sound of Your trumpets, Your angels, Your smoke, and Your fire, that we might fear You and be holy in Your presence. – Exodus 20:18

- Lord, send forth Your arrows, Your lightning bolts, and vanquish Your foes. – 2 Samuel 22:15

- Cover Your hands, Lord, with lightning, and command it to strike those who stand against us. – Job 36:32

- Hear our prayer, O Lord, let it come into Your ear. Let the earth shake and tremble by Your reply. Let smoke go up from Your nostrils and a devouring fire from Your mouth. Thunder from heaven, release hailstones and coals of fire, send out Your arrows, scatter the foe, with lightning in abundance vanquish them. – Psalm 18:6-14

The Sword

- "You will chase your enemies, and they shall fall by the sword before you. Five of you shall chase a hundred, and a hundred of you shall put ten thousand to flight; and your enemies shall fall by the sword before you." – Leviticus 26:7-8

- Let the Angel of the Lord draw His sword that we may fight with Him against our enemies and foes. – Numbers 22:23; Joshua 5:13

- I will now whet my glittering sword to render vengeance upon the enemies of the Lord. – Deuteronomy 32:41

- Lord Jesus, we understand You did not come to bring peace on the earth in this time, but a sword; therefore, we take up the sword of the Lord. – Matthew 10:34

- Lord, bend us like Judah, Your bow. Fit us as the double blessing of Ephraim, raise us up against the sons of carnality and unbelief to go forth with mighty power and wonders as the sword of a mighty man. – Zechariah 9:13

- We take the sword of the Spirit, which is the word of God, and go forth to establish His word on the earth.
  – Ephesians 6:17; Psalm 119

- Let now the Word penetrate like a sharp two-edged sword the heart and soul of this city, this region, and this place.
  – Hebrews 4:12

- I release the sword of the Lord against the powers of darkness in Jesus' name. – Judges 7:18

98

- Lord, gird Your sword on Your thigh and ride prosperously through the earth. – Psalm 45:3

- Let Your enemies in this place fall by the sword. – Psalm 63:10

- In Jesus' name, let the sword of the Lord go out against Leviathan; the false prophets of Jezebel, let them be executed. – Isaiah 27:1; 1 Kings 18:40

- Lord, release the sword out of Your mouth against the enemy. – Revelation 19:15

- "Let the high praises of God be in (our) mouths, and a two-edged sword in (our) hand, to execute vengeance on the nations, and punishments on the peoples; to bind their kings with chains, and their nobles with fetter of iron; to execute on them the written judgment – this honor have all His saints. Praise the Lord!" – Psalm 149:6-9

THE POWER OF GOD

- I am strong in the Lord and in the power of His might. – Ephesians 6:12

- Lord, display Your mighty power so men will believe. Release Your power in healing and deliverance. – Luke 5:17

- Let Your people be amazed at Your awesome power. – Luke 9:43

- Let signs, wonders, and miracles be released through the power of the Holy Spirit. – Romans 15:19

- Let me preach with a demonstration of power and of the Holy Spirit. – 1 Corinthians 2:4

- Holy Spirit, come upon me with power, that I may give witness to Christ's resurrection and victory over all the power of Satan. – Acts 1:8

- Release the power of the spirit of Elijah upon this generation. – Malachi 4:4; Luke 1:17

- Let Your glorious power be released against Your enemies. – Exodus 15:6

- Rule over Your enemies through Your great power. – Psalm 66:7

- I release the power and authority of the Lord against all demons and unclean spirits I encounter, in Jesus' name be gone! – Matthew 10:11

- I release furious rebukes upon the enemies of the Lord. – Ezekiel 25:17

- I release the battering ram against the gates of Hades. – Ezekiel 21:22

- Let the spirit of the Assyrians be broken in my land. – Isaiah 14:25

- Let a thousand flee at my rebuke, O Lord. – Isaiah 30:17

- Let the enemy perish at Your rebuke, O Lord. – Psalm 80:16

- The Lord has broken every yoke off my neck and burst every band, that I may serve Him; therefore, I loose every yoke and every band off my neck and my life in Jesus' name. – Jeremiah 30:8

- Let the oppressor in my land be broken in pieces. – Psalm 72:4

- Let the enemy's horse and rider, chariot and rider, captains and rulers that come against me be broken in pieces. – Jeremiah 51:21-23

- I break down every wall erected by the enemy against my life. – Hosea 10:12

- Lord, break in pieces the gates of brass, cut the bars of iron, and open the double gate, that Your treasure can come to me. – Isaiah 45:2-3

- I rebuke every enemy in the gates. – Psalm 127:5

- Open before me the gates, that I may go in and receive the blessings of the Lord; let all my gates be restored and repaired. – Nehemiah 3

- Lord, in Jesus' name I pray You will raise up bethel churches that will be the gate of heaven. – Genesis 28:17

- Let the gates of my life, my church, and my city open up for the King of glory to come in. – Psalm 24:7

- Let the foundations of the wicked be exposed and broken in this place. – Ezekiel 30:4

THE ARROWS

- I release the Lord's sharp arrows into the heart of the King's enemies. – Psalm 45:5

- Send forth Your arrow, O Lord, and scatter the enemy. – Psalm 18:14

- Shoot Your arrows and destroy them. – Psalm 144:6

- Make my enemies turn back because of the arrows on Your strings. – Psalm 21:12

- Shoot Your arrows upon those who devise shrewd schemes against me. Let them suddenly be wounded and flee away. – Psalm 64:7

- Break their bones and pierce them through with Your arrows. – Numbers 24:8

- Set Your mark upon my enemies for Your arrows. – Lamentations 3:12

- I release the arrow of the Lord's deliverance in my life. – 2 Kings 13:17

- Let the arrows of Ephraim release blessings through my life. – Zechariah 9:13

KINGDOM PRAYERS AND DECREES

- Father, we pray Your Kingdom come and Your will be done on earth, this earth where I live, just as it is in heaven.
  – Matthew 6:10

- Let Your Kingdom advance and be established through preaching the gospel of the Kingdom, through power encounters, deliverance, and victories confirmed by signs, wonders, and miracles. – Matthew 4:23-25

- Let men bless the Lord in all places of His dominion.
  – Psalm 103:22

- Lord, "Your kingdom is an everlasting kingdom, and Your dominion endures throughout all generations." Let Your dominion be demonstrated in our generations. – Psalm 145:13

- Let men know Your mighty acts and the glorious majesty of Your Kingdom. – Psalm 145:12

- Let men speak of the glory of Your Kingdom and talk of Your power. – Psalm 145:11

- Let the righteousness, peace, and joy of the Kingdom fill our lives and this place, by the Holy Spirit. – Romans 14:17

- Let the scepter of Your Kingdom be released through Your righteous saints; overturn the thrones of wicked kingdoms.
  – Hebrews 1:8; Haggai 2:22

- Break in pieces and consume every demonic kingdom that resists Your dominion. – Psalm 72:8

- Father, I receive Your Kingdom because it is Your good pleasure to give it to me. – Luke 12:32

- I seek first the Kingdom of God and His righteousness, and all things regarding food, clothing, shelter, and increase of human needs are added unto me. – Matthew 6:33

Apostolic Prayers

- Let the eyes of my understanding be enlightened that I might know what is the hope of Your calling, what are the riches of the glory of Your inheritance in the saints, and what is the exceeding greatness of Your power toward us who believe.
  – Ephesians 1:17-19

- Christ Jesus, come and dwell in my heart by faith, and let me be rooted and grounded in love; let me comprehend with all the saints what is the breadth, length, depth, and height of Your love, that I may be filled with the fullness of God.
  – Ephesians 3:17-18

- Let me be filled with the knowledge of Your will in all wisdom and spiritual understanding, that I might walk worthy of the Lord, pleasing Him, being fruitful in every good work and increasing in the knowledge of God. – Colossians 1:9-10

- Let Your word have free access to all my life.
  – 2 Thessalonians 3:11

- Let me be one with my fellow believers, that the world will believe I have been sent by You. – John 17:21

- Let my love abound more and more in all wisdom and knowledge. – Philippians 1:9

- Let me know Jesus, the power of His resurrection, and the fellowship of His sufferings, being made conformable to His death. – Philippians 3:10

- Let me be strengthened with all might, according to His glorious power, unto all patience and longsuffering with joyfulness. – Colossians 1:11

- Strengthen me with might by Your Spirit in the inner man. – Ephesians 3:16

- My heart and desire, my prayer, is for all Israel to be saved. – Romans 10:1

CHAPTER TEN

PROVISION, PROMISES, PRAYERS AND PURSUITS

PROSPERITY AND FINANCES

- God has given me all things that pertain to life and godliness. I am a partaker of His divine nature and I am well able to possess all God has provided for me. – 2 Peter 1:3-4; Numbers 13:30

- The blessing of the Lord makes one truly rich and He adds no sorrow to it. – Proverbs 10:22

- The Lord has commanded the blessing on me and in my storehouses, and all to which I have set my hand, my life and land is blessed. My bank accounts are full, my health is excellent, and my life is abundantly supplied. – Deuteronomy 28:8

- God delights in my prosperity and gives me the power to get wealth, that I may establish His covenant in the earth. – Deuteronomy 8:18; 11:12

- God makes all grace abound toward me; therefore I have all sufficiency for all things at all times, and I abound in every good work. – 2 Corinthians 9:8

- There is no lack in my life, for my God supplies all my need according to His riches in glory by Christ Jesus.
  – Philippians 4:19

- Because I tithe faithfully, the Lord rebukes the devourer for my sake. – Malachi 3:10-11

- I have been given the authority to bind and loose, therefore I bind the spirit of poverty and destruction against my life. In Jesus' name I loose abundant finances, blessings, increase, and wealth to come to me by the authority and grace of God.
  – Matthew 16:19

- The Lord takes pleasure in the prosperity of His servants, and the blessings of Abraham are mine.
  – Psalm 35:27; Galatians 3:14

- Lord, I seek first Your Kingdom and Your righteousness, that all my basic needs You will add to me. – Matthew 6:33

- Lord, I believe Your word: As I give it, it shall be given unto me, good measure, pressed down, shaken together and running over shall be released upon me! – Luke 6:38

- Lord, cause my soul to prosper, that I may be in good health and prosper in all things. – 3 John 2

BLESSING AND FAVOR

- This is my set time for favor. – Psalm 102:13

- Lord, I entreat Your favor. – Psalm 45:12

- Be favorable unto my land, and let my horn be exalted.
  – Psalm 85:1; 89:17

- Lord, I entreat Your favor with my whole heart. – Psalm 119:58

- Let Your favor be upon my life as a cloud of the latter rain.
  – Proverbs 16:15

- Let Your beauty be upon my life and let me be well favored.
  – Genesis 29:17

- Lord, I know You favor me, because my enemies do not triumph
  over me. – Psalm 41:11

- Let me be satisfied with favor, and filled with Your blessing.
  – Deuteronomy 33:23

- Lord, bless my latter end more than my beginning. – Job 42:12

- Thank You for Your mercies that are new every morning; You
  daily load me with benefits. – Lamentations 3:23; Psalm 68:19

- By Your favor, Lord, let my mountain stand strong. – Psalm 30:7

- Lord, bless me, and cause Your face to shine upon me, that
  Your way may be known upon the earth and Your saving health
  among all nations. Let my land yield its increase, its harvest, its
  blessing, and let the ends of the earth fear You. – Psalm 67

STRENGTH

- I shall arise and go in the strength of the Lord. – Psalm 71:16

- I shall be wise and strong; as I increase in knowledge and wisdom, I will increase in strength. – Proverbs 24:5

- Lord, You have made me stronger than my enemies. – Psalm 105:24

- Lord, You have made me bold with strength in my soul. – Psalm 138:3

- O God, because I have waited on You, I will mount up with wings like an eagle, I will run and not be weary, walk and not faint. – Isaiah 40:31

- You are my strength and my song. Lord, You have become my salvation. – Psalm 118:14

- You have commanded my strength. O God, strengthen that which You have done for me. – Psalm 68:28

- "My flesh and my heart fail; but God is the strength of my heart and my portion forever." – Psalm 73:26

- Lord, You strengthen me with Your mouth. – Job 16:5

- Lord, You are my strength and my shield. – Psalm 28:7

- I will strengthen myself in the Lord. – 1 Samuel 30:6

- I will be strong and courageous, that I may observe to do all the Lord has commanded, that I may always prosper. – Joshua 1:6-8

- Your grace is sufficient for me, Your strength is made perfect in my weakness. – 2 Corinthians 12:9

- I will be strong in the Lord and in the power of His might. – Ephesians 6:10

- I am strengthened with might through His Spirit in the inner man. – Ephesians 3:16

- I will not waver at the promise of God through unbelief, but I will be strengthened in faith, giving glory to God. – Romans 4:20

- Lord, Your energy works in me mightily. – Colossians 1:29

- I can do all things through Christ who strengthens me. – Philippians 4:13

- The joy of the Lord is my strength, therefore I will be strong in the grace that is in Christ Jesus. – Nehemiah 8:10, 2 Timothy 2:1

INCREASE AND ENLARGEMENT

- Let me increase with the increase of God, let me increase exceedingly; increase my greatness and comfort me on every side. – Colossians 2:19; Genesis 30:43; Psalm 71:21

- In Jesus' name, I break off any limitations and barriers placed on my life by the works of darkness and evil spirits. I bind up and cast off all python and restricting spirits, for God did not give me a spirit of fear, but of power, love, and a sound mind. – Romans 8:15; 2 Timothy 1:7

- The Lord shall increase me more and more, me and my children. – Psalm 115:14

- I ask to be filled with the Holy Spirit: the Spirit of the Lord, the Spirit of wisdom and understanding, the Spirit of counsel and might, the Spirit of knowledge and fear of the Lord. – Ephesians 5:18; Isaiah 11:2

- Now I can do all things through Christ who strengthens me, I can do exceedingly abundantly above all that I ask or think according to the power that works in us, the power of the Holy Spirit. – Philippians 4:13; Ephesians 3:20-21

- Lord, cast out my enemies and enlarge my borders. Lord you have promised to enlarge my borders. – Ezekiel 34:34; Deuteronomy 12:20

- Enlarge my heart so I can run the way of Your commandments; enlarge my steps so I can receive Your wealth and prosperity. – Psalm 119:32; Isaiah 60:5-9

- Lord, let me increase in wisdom and stature and in favor with God and with man. – Luke 2:52

- Let my faith grow; let me grow in grace and in the knowledge of the Lord Jesus Christ. – 2 Thessalonians 1:3; 2 Peter 3:18

- Let me increase in strength and confound my adversaries. – Acts 9:22

- Let the increase of Your government and peace, O Lord, come into and through my life. – Isaiah 9:6-7

- I will flourish like a palm tree and grow like a cedar in Lebanon. I'm a tree planted by the rivers of water that brings forth fruit in its season, whose leaf also shall not wither; and whatever I do will prosper. God will even turn my mistakes around and cause me to prosper. – Psalm 92:12; Psalm 1:3

DELIVERANCE

- Jesus, You went about doing good and healing all those oppressed by the devil. Lord, undertake for me against all my oppressors. – Acts 10:38; Isaiah 38:14

- Deliver me from the oppressors that seek after my soul. Break in pieces the oppressor. – Psalm 54:3; 72:4

- I rebuke and cast out all spirits of affliction and oppression that work at bringing me down, in Jesus' name. – Psalm 107:39

- I rebuke the voice of the oppressor in my midst. – Psalm 55:3

- I break every written curse that has come upon my life in Jesus' name. – 2 Chronicles 34:24

- I break every anointed curse against my life by the spirit of Balaam, in Jesus' name. – Nehemiah 13:2

- I break all generation curses off my life and body. I break all generational rebellion that would cause me to resist the Holy Spirit. – Galatians 3:13; Acts 7:51

- I rebuke in Jesus' name the spirit of poverty – be cast out. No enemy shall take my inheritance through oppression. – Ecclesiastes 5:8; Ezekiel 46:18

- Lord, You are my refuge from the oppressor; execute judgment against them. – Psalm 9:9; 146:7

- I rebuke all spirits of madness and confusion in Jesus' name. I rule over my oppressors. – Ecclesiastes 7:7; Psalm 14:2

- Deliver me, O Lord, out of the hand of my enemies. Make haste and deliver me in Your righteousness. – Psalm 70:1; 71:2-4

- Deliver me from the oppression of man, from lying lips, and a deceitful tongue. – Psalm 119:134; 120:2

- Deliver me from my fears, from all my troubles. Deliver me from those who hate me. Deliver my soul from death, my eyes from tears, and my feet from falling.
  – Psalm 34:4; 54:7; 69:14; 116:8

- Let miracles of deliverance be in my life. – Daniel 6:27

- I renounce and break all ungodly oaths and allegiances made by my ancestors to idols, demons, false religions, and ungodly organizations. – Matthew 5:33; Ezekiel 23;32

- I loose myself from the spirit of the world, the lust of the flesh, and the pride of life. Depart from me in Jesus' name! I overcome the world by the power of the Holy Spirit. – 1 John 2:16

- I declare no evil will touch me; shame to those who wish me evil, I will not be visited with evil. – Job 5:19; Psalm 40:14; Proverbs 19:23

- I keep my feet from every evil path so I might keep Your Word. Deliver me from evil, preserve me from evil.
  – Psalm 119:101; 121:7

- I will not be overcome by evil, rather I will overcome evil with good. – Romans 12:21

- I command every unclean demonic spirit operating in any area of my body, my mind, my will, and my emotions to come out and depart from me in Jesus Christ's mighty name. Lord, let Your healing and restoration now come forth in all areas, to Your glory, power, and dominion.

PROTECTION

- Lord, You make me to dwell safely; keep me as the apple of Your eye, hide me under the shadow of Your wings. In the shadow of Your wings I trust. – Psalm 4:8; 17:8; 57:1

- The name of the Lord is a strong tower, I run into it and I'm safe. I will dwell in safety, nothing shall make me afraid. – Proverbs 18:10; Ezekiel 34:28

- Let the angel of the Lord encamp around me and protect me. Be my defense and my refuge. – Psalm 34:7; 59:16

- Lord, You are my shield and my hiding place. Let Your truth be my shield, let Your glory be my defense; the name of the Lord is a strong tower. I run into it and I'm safe. – Psalm 119:114; Isaiah 4:5; Proverbs 18:10

- I will not be afraid of ten thousand that have set themselves against me, because You are a shield for me. – Psalm 3:1-6

- "When the enemy comes in like a flood, the Spirit of the Lord will lift up a standard against him." – Isaiah 59:19

- When my ways please the Lord, He will make even my enemies to be at peace with me. – Proverb 16:7

- "Though I walk in the midst of trouble, You will revive me; You will stretch out Your hand against the wrath of my enemies, and Your right hand will save me." – Psalm 138:7

HEALTH

- Bless the Lord, O my soul, and forget not all His benefits: who forgives all my iniquities, who heals all my diseases, who redeems my life from destruction, who crowns me with lovingkindness and tender mercies, who satisfies my mouth with good things, so that my youth is renewed like the eagle's. – Psalm 103:1-5

- "My son, give attention to my words; incline your ear to my sayings. Do not let them depart from your eyes; keep them in the midst of your heart; for they are life to those who find them, and health to all their flesh." – Proverbs 4:20-22

- "If you diligently heed the voice of the Lord your God and do what is right in His sight, give ear to His commandments and keep all His statutes, I will put none of the diseases on you which I have brought on the Egyptians. For I am the Lord who heals you." – Exodus 15:26

- "Surely He has borne our griefs and carried our sorrows; yet we esteemed Him stricken, smitten by God, and afflicted. But He was wounded for our transgressions, He was bruised for iniquities; the chastisement for our peace was upon Him, and by His stripes we are healed." – Isaiah 53:4-5

Under the old covenant, healing and health were the blessing of the Lord, the blessing of obedience. Sickness was a result of disobedience. If one disobeyed, they came under the curse of the law, which included sickness, poverty, and death (Deuteronomy 28).

- Now Christ has become a curse for me. He has released me from the curse of the law. I am now the righteousness of God in Christ, free from the curse, free from sickness, disease, poverty, and death. – Galatians 3:13

- I rebuke the curse of sickness from my body. – Deuteronomy 28

> Blindness – 28:29
>
> Boils – 28:35
>
> Consumption (Tuberculosis) – 28:22
>
> Fever – 28:22
>
> Inflammation – 28:22
>
> Itching – 28:27
>
> Mental illness – 28:28
>
> Scabs – 28:27
>
> Plague – 28:21
>
> Hemorrhoids – 28:27
>
> Tumors – 28:27
>
> All diseases – 28:29

- I rebuke the spirit of infirmity from my body in Jesus' name.

- It's God's desire that I be in health and prosper, even as my soul prospers. – 3 John 1:2

- Jesus, You bore my griefs, You paid the penalty for my sickness and disease and carried it far from me. You carried away my sorrows, my pains, and afflictions; therefore, in Jesus' name I am healed. – Matthew 8:17; 1 Peter 2:24

- God, You revealed that You are my healer; therefore, Lord, I will entreat You that You might see me and heal me, that You will restore physical comfort to me.
  – Exodus 15:26; Isaiah 19:22, 57:18

- I will arise and bless the Lord for keeping every disease from me.
  – Deuteronomy 7:13-15

- Lord, I believe Your promise; my health is restored and my wounds are healed. – Jeremiah 30:17; Matthew 8:7

- You have brought health to me and cured me. I have an abundance of peace and truth. – Jeremiah 33:6

- I shall live and have life in my spirit. God has delivered me from corruption. – Isaiah 38:16-20

- Lord, bless my bread and water and take sickness away from me. – Exodus 23:25

- Listen, O Lord I pray, and heal me. Have mercy on me, for I am weak; heal me, for my bones are weak. – 2 Chronicles 30:20; Psalm 6:2

- Lord, send Your word and heal me! – Psalm 107:20

- Heal me, O Lord, and I shall be healed; let Your virtue touch my life and heal me. – Jeremiah 17:14; Luke 6:19

- I command every organ in my body to function perfectly the way God intended. – Psalm 139:14

- Lord, keep all my bones; let them become healthy because I receive the good report of the gospel.
  – Psalm 34:20; Proverbs 15:30

- I pray for my immune system to be strengthened in the name of Jesus. – Psalm 119:28

- My flesh shall be fresher than a young child and I will return to the days of my youth. – Job 33:25

- No sickness or plague shall come near my home. – Psalm 91:10

- Jesus, arise over my life with healing in Your wings. – Malachi 4:2

- Lord, sustain me and strengthen me on my bed of illness. – Psalm 41:3

- The Lord will bind up my bruise and heal the stroke of my wound. – Isaiah 30:26

- Jesus, You make me whole, You are the strength of my life. – Acts 9:34; Psalm 27:1

- No sickness I am healed from shall come upon me a second time. I rebuke you in Jesus' name. Go out and go away. I make an utter end to you. – Nahum 1:9

- "But let a man examine himself, and so let him eat of the bread and drink the cup. For he who eats and drinks in an unworthy manner eats and drinks judgment to himself, not discerning the Lord's body. For this reason many are weak and sick among you, and many sleep." Lord, forgive me for not correctly discerning Your body, Your brethren; forgive my judgmental, divisive, and selfish ways. Let wrong judgment now be released from my body; let sickness and weakness now leave. Let strength and healing come in Jesus' name. – 1 Corinthians 11:17-34

- The Lord will restore health to me and heal me of all my wounds. – Jeremiah 30:17

SOUL HARVEST

Therefore, if anyone is in Christ, he is a new creation; old things have passed away; behold, all things have become new. Now all things are of God, who has reconciled us to Himself through Jesus Christ, and has given us the ministry of reconciliation, that is, that God was in Christ reconciling the world to Himself, not imputing their trespasses to them, and has committed to us the word of reconciliation. Now then, we are ambassadors for Christ, as though God were pleading through us: we implore you on Christ's behalf, be reconciled to God (2 Corinthians 5:17-20).

- The earth is Yours, O Lord, and all its fullness, the world and those who dwell therein. Let the souls of all men in this place turn and hear Your Word; let them be saved and healed. – Psalm 24:1

- Behold all souls are Yours, O Lord: the soul of the father as well as the soul of the son. Let us arise in the spirit of Elijah and restore the hearts of the fathers to the sons and the hearts of the sons to the fathers, lest the soul that sins shall die. – Ezekiel 18:4; Malachi 4:6

- Lord, You are against the magic seductions of evil that hunt souls of men like birds. Tear the captivated souls from the snare of the fowler, remove their veil that they might see and be saved. – Ezekiel 13:20

- In Jesus' name, I loose and free the souls of men in my area from divination and witchcraft. I bind the hunter of souls here! – Ezekiel 13:23

- Let men say their soul has escaped as a bird out of the snare of the fowler. – Psalm 124:7

- The harvest is plentiful, but the laborers are few. Therefore we pray the Lord of the harvest to send laborers into the harvest. – Matthew 9:37-38

- Let the Kingdom of heaven be established in this place, let the people go forth and sow good seed in their field for harvest. – Matthew 13:24

- Lord, command Your angels that reap and gather to come now into the harvest field. Let them help us with the harvest as they did Phillip, to separate and reap sons of the Kingdom. – Matthew 13:30; Acts 8:26-36

- Let our food be the will of the Lord who sends us! Behold we lift up our eyes and look at the fields, for they are already ripe for harvest. We shall go forth and reap and receive wages and gather fruit for eternal life. – John 4:34-36

- "Behold, I will send for many fishermen," says the Lord, "and they shall fish them; and afterward I will send for many hunters, and they shall hunt them from every mountain and every hill, and out of the holes of the rocks." – Jeremiah 16:16

- Lord, let us be willing to leave the 99 righteous and go after the one who is lost, until we find him. Let us successfully return, rejoicing at their salvation. Let heaven rejoice with us! – Luke 15:4-7

- Lord, we now call all the guests to the great supper for all things are now ready. – Luke 14:7

- Lord, give us grace and strength to go out into the highways and hedges to compel them to come in, that Your house may be filled. – Luke 14:23

- Lord, I planted, others have watered, but You give the increase. Lord, cause now Your increase to come to our harvest, we ask in Jesus' name. – 1 Corinthians 3:6-7

- Let us go forth with great power, filled with the Holy Spirit, moving among the people with healing, deliverance, signs and wonders, turning whole cities and multitudes to You. – Acts 2-3

- Holy Spirit, come upon me with great power, that I may bring forth the witness of Christ's victory over all the powers of darkness. – Acts 1:8; Colossians 2:15

- Lord, I ask You for this nation, for my inheritance, the souls of men, and the defeat of my enemies. – Psalms 2:8

- Lord, You chose me and appointed me that I should go and bear fruit, and that my fruit should remain. Therefore, Father, I ask in Jesus' name to be abundantly fruitful in the harvest, bringing forth fruit that remains. – John 15:16

- Let people come to me and ask me about the Kingdom of God. Let the whosoevers come, believe, and be born again. Let Your love permeate this place. – John 3:1-16

CHAPTER ELEVEN

PRAYER AND PROCLAMATIONS FOR THE NATIONS

- I pray my nation will bring forth the praises of God. – Isaiah 60:6

- I pray my nation will seek the Lord and enter into His rest. – Isaiah 11:10

- Lord, I ask that You do a new thing in my nation by giving water in the wilderness and streams in the desert. – Isaiah 43:19-20

- I pray the children of my nation will be taught of the Lord. – Isaiah 54:13

- Lord, I pray my nation will be saved and walk in the light. – Revelation 21:24

- Lord, I pray my nation will look to you and be saved. – Isaiah 45:22

- I pray the people who walk in darkness in my nation will see the light and let your light shine on those in darkness. – Isaiah 9:2

- I pray my nation will be given to the rule and reign of the Lord. – Daniel 7:14

- Let the Kingdom of God be manifest in my nation in righteousness, peace, and joy in the Holy Spirit. – Romans 14:17

- Let your glory be declared among my people, and Your great wonders be done in my nation. – Psalm 96:3

- Let my nation praise the Lord for His lovingkindness, mercy, and truth. – Psalm 117

- I pray for the poor and needful in my nation, that they would be delivered. – Psalm 72:12-13

- My nation is the Lord's and all its fullness, the people and all that dwell there. – Psalm 24:1

- Let the Lord's dominion be established in my nation and let His enemies lick the dust. – Psalm 72:8-9

- Lord, let all the idolaters in my nation be confounded and the gods turn and worship You. – Psalm 97:7

- Let the wicked in my nation be cut down and wither as the green herb. – Psalm 37:2

- Let every covenant with death and hell be broken in my nation. – Isaiah 28:18

- Let the wicked be rooted out of my land. – Proverbs 2:22

- I pray my nation will make a joyful noise to the Lord and serve Him with gladness. – Psalm 100:1-2

- Let my nation be filled with the knowledge of the glory of the Lord, as the waters cover the seas. – Habakkuk 2:14

PRAYERS FOR AMERICA

- Let all America fear the Lord. Let all the inhabitants of the United States stand in awe of Him. Blessed is the nation whose God is the Lord, and the people whom He has chosen as His own inheritance. – Psalm 33:8,12

- We praise and thank You for our president. We pray that he will seek Your wisdom and counsel in all his actions on behalf of this country, and in his personal and private life. – Psalm 89:21

- Lord, act in Your own displeasure toward those who would strike terror into the earth. Root out and bring terrorists to justice. Please show mercy, expose and thwart terrorist schemes. Grant wisdom, discernment, and protection to all in authority working to prevent terrorist attacks.
  – Ezekiel 32:22-25; Psalm 7:11-16

- We pray that You would give Your wisdom to those who would preside in our courts of justice. Let all judges and those who work in our court system seek to preserve justice in a fair and impartial way according to Your statutes. – Proverbs 2:6-8

- Grant wisdom and courage to all those who serve in our Congress, and all elected officials across this country. Let them not be distracted from governing by the lure of money, power or fame. Encourage them to always stand for what is right and to faithfully serve those who have put their trust in them.
  – Ecclesiastes 8:1-5

- Let those who serve our country in the military not rely solely upon the strength of their weapons and intelligence, but first turn to You, Lord, the source of all wisdom and strength. Raise up men and women of faith among all ranks of the military and give them opportunity to witness to their fellow soldiers.
  – Matthew 8:5-12

- We agree with You, Jesus, that the church will be one, as You are one with the Father. Heal any divisions that exist between pastors and their congregations, and between denominations. Let our nation see the body of Christ united in love for one another, and toward those whom You have come to save.
  – John 17:21

- Lord, return the state of marriage to a place of honor in our country. We praise You for sturdy marriages that model Your commitment to the church. Let hope and healing now come to those marriages that are strained and breaking. – Hebrews 13:4

- Father, let our earthly fathers look to You as the ultimate spiritual head of the family, and serve their families by carrying the responsibility for the physical, emotional, and spiritual well-being of their wives and children. Bring absentee fathers to a faith and radical life-change. Let Your character be clearly seen in the lives of all fathers. – Ephesians 6:4

- We ask You, Lord, to refresh mothers in the honor of fulfilling the glory of motherhood. Strengthen them with grace, wisdom, and love in serving their husbands and children. Let mothers reflect Your own love and nurturing nature.
  – Proverbs 31:25-26,28

- Thank You for being a father to the fatherless and husband to the widow. Restore our broken families with Your wholeness and let them turn to You for all spiritual, emotional, and physical needs. – Psalm 146:8-9

- We pray that our children will come to know You as Lord and Savior early in their lifetime. We pray that they would participate fully in establishing Your Kingdom here on earth. – Mark 10:14

- We agree with Your Word, Lord, that You are instructing our children, and great will be their peace in the land. – Isaiah 54:13

- Let the unborn be protected. We affirm their personhood and we honor them as unborn citizens. Rescue them from the atrocity and violent death by abortion. Convict of transgression, forgive and heal those who repent of committing abortion.
  – Psalm 72:12,14

- Lord, we implore You to make our schools a place where our children can learn in physical, emotional, and spiritual safety. Give them godly teachers who encourage them and are dedicated to them. Give them the support systems at home and at school that would enable them to achieve great things in Your Name. – Luke 6:40

- Strengthen and encourage those in the media who are willing to stand for Your truth and practice honest, fair, and accurate reporting. Convert or remove those who would use the media to put forth their own selfish agendas and proclaim their lies and distortions. Give discernment to all who know and love You to be able to sit through the untruths and rely on Your steadfast Word. – Proverbs 4:24-26

- We praise and thank You that You give us the arts as a way to worship and glorify Your Name. Let godly men and women now come forth in the arts and entertainment fields who will seek to share Your gospel message through their creative endeavors. – Proverbs 14:34

- Lord, bring genuine reconciliation to the races of this nation. Remove long held prejudices, hatreds, and hurts and replace them with Your healing love and fellowship. Bring peace, friendship, and equal opportunity to all peoples and cultures. – Ephesians 2:14-16

- Thank You that You do not forget prisoners and those who are homeless and needy. Stir up Your heart of compassion in each of us and send Your Spirit to guide us as we reach out to those less fortunate. – Psalm 107:41

- Restore our abandoned inner cities to communities of safety, prosperity, and hope. Save and encourage those caught in cycles of poverty, sickness, addiction, brokenness, and despair. – Isaiah 58:12

- Lord, grant the people of America sabbath rest. Thank You that there remains therefore a rest for the people of God. Help all to be diligent to enter that rest, lest anyone fall into disobedience. – Hebrews 4:9-11

- Lord, let all exhausted laborers in our land come to You, find salvation, and find rest for their souls, for Your yoke is easy and Your burden is light. Comfort those in jail and prison, Lord. – Matthew 11:18-30

- Shield and deliver our nation from occultism, New Age cults, false religions, and secret societies. – Isaiah 1:29; 2:6

- Lord, bring the Word of God to bear on the hearts and minds of those who make public policy in America. Continue to grant opportunity for a biblical world view and principles into the public discourse. – Psalm 19:7-11; John 8:31,32; Ephesians 3:10

- In mercy, reveal Yourself to those who do not even seek after You, those who have turned away, and those who are ignorant of their own need for Your saving grace in their lives.
  – Romans 10:20; Isaiah 65:1

- Reverse the trends of humanism and socialism in our nation.
  – 1 Chronicles 12:32; Isaiah 59:15

- Help us to be a nation that desires purity and avoids debauchery, pornography, perversion, drunkenness, drug use and gambling.
  – 1 Corinthians 6:9-20; Titus 2:12

- Grace and enable us, Lord, to travail until the fullness of Jesus Christ is birthed in this next generation of Americans.
  – Galatians 4:19

- Send forth more consecrated individuals to proclaim the gospel of Jesus Christ to every nation. Bring in the harvest, Lord.
  – Acts 1:8; 4:33

- Lord, help us to live our lives so that all are prepared to give an account to Almighty God. – Hebrews 9:27

- Now to Him who is able to keep us from falling, and to present us faultless before the presence of His glory with exceeding joy, to the only wise God our Savior, be glory and majesty, dominion and power, both now and forever. Amen. – Jude 1:24-25

PRAYERS FOR ISRAEL

- Father God, remove the veil You have sovereignly placed over the eyes of Israel, that they would recognize Jesus as their Messiah. – 2 Corinthians 3:14

- Lord, show Your mercy and favor to Israel in this set time. – Psalm 102:13

- We pray for the current leaders in Israel, including the prime minister, the mayor of Jerusalem, and all those in military service. Raise up government leaders in Israel (and worldwide) who will not seek to "divide the land," and who would recognize the unique significance of Jerusalem in God's end-time purposes.

- "He who scattered Israel will gather him, and keep him as a shepherd does his flock." Father, continue to draw the Jewish people to You according to Your sovereign plan. – Jeremiah 31:10

- Let them all be confounded and turned back that hate Zion. Let them be as grass upon the housetops, which withers before it grows up. Lord, deal justly and swiftly with Your enemies. – Psalm 129:5-6

- Destroy and divide tongues of those who would incite violence against Israel. In the name of Jesus, we bind every false religion and false doctrine that does not acknowledge Your eternal plan for the land and people of Israel. – Psalm 55:9

- The scepter of the wicked will not remain over the land allotted to the righteous. Father, break strongholds of religion, pride, and wickedness that seek to control Israel. – Psalm 125:3

- "For the Lord will not forsake His people, for His great name's sake, because it has pleased the Lord to make (Israel) His people. Use us to help others understand Your plan for Israel and Your love for the Jewish people. – 1 Samuel 12:22

- "The Lord brings the counsel of the nations to nothing; He makes the plans of the peoples of no effect." We declare that God's purpose for Israel will be completely fulfilled and that He will be glorified. – Psalm 33:10

- Show Your lovingkindness to Your people Israel and keep them as the apple of Your eye. Hide them under the shadow of Your wings from the wicked who oppress them and from their deadly enemies who surround them. – Psalm 17:7-9

- We pray that You would remember your covenants and promises towards Israel, especially when others rise up against her to swallow her alive. When their wrath is kindled against her, the waters will not overwhelm her. God will not give her as prey to their teeth. – Psalm 124

- Sanctify Your great name which has been profaned among the nations, which has been profaned in the midst of Israel, that nations shall know that the Lord is God, when He is sanctified in Israel before their eyes. Sprinkle the clean water of Your Word on Israel and cleanse her from her filthiness and from all her idols, including abortion and the occult. Give Israel a new heart, and put a new spirit within her. Remove her heart of stone and give her a heart of flesh that can respond to the Holy Spirit and cause her to walk in Your statutes, keep Your commandments and do them. – Ezekiel 36:23-27

- Cause the church to fulfill its commission to preach the Gospel to the whole world, so the full number of the Gentiles would come into the kingdom. Then all Israel will be saved.
  – Romans 11:25-26

- We pray for the peace of Jerusalem and for it to remain Israel's undivided capital. – Psalm 122:6

- Father, in Your mercy vanquish the tremendously powerful religious spirits which dominate the whole territory; Jewish, Christian, and others.

- We pray for a spirit of unity, for peace between religious and secular Jews, for peace to exist among believers in the land.

- We pray for the body of the Messiah in Israel to become a praying, maturing body. We pray that this body would allow the love and compassion of Yeshua to flow through them and touch everyone they encounter.

- Raise up intercessors for Israel. Put more watchmen on the walls of Jerusalem who would give You no peace day or night until You establish Jerusalem and make her the praise of the earth.
  – Isaiah 62:6-7

- Father, bring glory to Your name through the mercy You show to the land. Bring the necessary seasonal rain upon the country. Cause the crops to be bountiful.

- We pray that the three spiritual forces of humanism, Marxist socialist philosophy, and the spiritual inheritance of the Ottoman Empire will be broken and rendered powerless.

- Bless Israel through the many immigrants who are flowing back to the nation. Bring sovereign, supernatural moves of the Holy Spirit among these new immigrants, that they might proclaim Your truth to their fellow Jews.

- We pray for a radical change in the Israeli system of government, that divisiveness and partisanship would give way to unity and cooperation; grant wisdom and revelation to all members of the Knesset and Israel's Supreme Court.

- We pray that, in the midst of the pressures, the people of Israel will turn to You, God. We pray that You will hear the heart cries of people in this land and have mercy. As it says in Isaiah 30:19, "You shall weep no more, He will be very gracious to you at the sound of your cry; when He hears it, He will answer you."

- Pour out Your Spirit upon the people of Israel, especially upon the young people, so that Your works can be declared to future generations.

- Raise up "sons of Zion" who take God's Word seriously in opposition to the humanistic "sons of Greece." – Zechariah 9:13

- We pray for the Holy Spirit to intervene in the current situation in Israel. "When the enemy comes in like a flood, the Spirit of the Lord will lift up a standard against him." – Isaiah 59:19

- Turn the hearts of the people of Israel to trust in the name of the Lord for deliverance, not in the chariots and horses of their military might. – Zechariah 4:6

- God, raise up elders and young leaders to teach and train the new generation of Israelis who are coming to faith in the Messiah.

- We pray that the Palestinian Arabs will come to faith in Christ and embrace God's end-time purpose for Israel; send forth laborers to bring in the appointed harvest from the whole of the Middle East.

- May Israel's relationship with the United States be strong, and may our nation, especially young believers, recognize and support God's purposes for Israel.

- Lord, we ask that young believers in America would come to love the Jewish people as they seek to prepare the way for the return of the Messiah.

    These prayers were from Derek Prince and can be found at www.prayerforallpeople.com/jerusalem.html

CHAPTER TWELVE

MINISTRY PREPARATION AND MEDITATIONS

- I am strengthened with all might according to His glorious power. – Colossians 1:10-11

- I am complete in Him, who is the head of all principality and power. – Colossians 2:10

- I am able in Christ to bring forth the increase of God's government and peace. – Isaiah 9:6-7

- I am chosen, anointed and appointed by Christ to be fruitful, bringing forth fruit that remains. – John 15:16

- I have world-overcoming faith residing on the inside of me. – 1 John 5:4-5; 1 John 4:4

- No weapon formed against me shall prosper, and every tongue that rises against me in judgment I condemn. – Isaiah 54:17

- No corrupt communication shall proceed out of my mouth, but what is good for necessary edification, that it may impart grace to the hearers. – Ephesians 4:29

- I will not grieve or quench the Holy Spirit. – Ephesians 4:30

- My hand is upon the neck of my enemies and I shall prevail. – Genesis 49:8

- God is with me; He is on my side, who can be against me? – Romans 8:31

- God did not spare His own Son, therefore He shall also freely give me all things. – Romans 8:32

- I am not just an overcomer, I am more than a conqueror through Him who loves me. – Romans 8:37

- I have authority over all the power of the enemy. I will tread on snakes and scorpions and over all the power of the enemy, and nothing by any means shall hurt me. – Luke 10:19

- I am strengthened with might by His Spirit in the inner man. – Ephesians 3:16

- These signs will follow me because I believe; I will cast out demons, speak with new tongues of men and angels, take up serpents, deal with crafty deception, and drink deadly things without hurt or harm. I will lay hands on the sick and they shall recover. – Mark 16: 17-18

- The breaker has gone up before me and broken through every limitation and barrier of the enemy. – Micah 2:13

- I can run through a troop and leap over a wall in the strength of the Lord. – Psalm 18:29

- Let the gospel be preached through me with signs and wonders following, stretch out your mighty hand to heal through your holy servant Jesus! – Acts 4:29-30

- Let men know Your mighty acts and glorious majesty of Your kingdom – Psalm 145:12

- Let my line go through all the earth and the words You give to me to the ends of the world. – Psalm 19:4

- I pray my speaking and ministering will make known the mysteries of the gospel and mysteries of Your will. – Ephesians 1:7-9

- I pray to receive dreams, visions, and revelations of the Lord in abundance. Let me be a good steward of Your revelations speaking forth the mysteries of Christ. – Colossians 4:3

- Father, let Your glory be revealed in my life. – John 12:28

- Let me understand things kept secret from the foundation of the world, that they may be made known to others. – Matthew 13:35

- Reveal to me secret and deep things. – Daniel 2:22

- Let me speak to others by revelation. – 1 Corinthians 14:6

- Let Your living Word and Your burden for Your people come forth, that I may speak and prophesy powerfully.

- Reveal and release the scepter of Your kingdom, the scepter of righteousness. – Hebrews 1:8

- I thank You, Lord, as I abide in Jesus and His words abide in me, I can ask what I desire and it shall be done for me. – John 15:7

- I am fully convinced that what God has promised He is able to perform. – Romans 4:21

- Let the plowman overtake the reaper in my life and ministry, the treader of grapes overtake the sower of seed, that I may see a continual harvest. – Amos 9:13

- God has given me dominion in every place I go. No man can keep me from my calling, my success or my inheritance. Take Your glory, Lord! – Joshua 1:3-5

- Jesus, You said the works You do, I shall do also, because I have received the promise of the Father, the Holy Spirit. Come, Holy Spirit, and give me power to witness. Fill me up.
  – John 14:12; Acts 1:8

- The Kingdom of God is within me. – Luke 17:21

- Let signs, wonders, and miracles be released through the power of the Holy Spirit, so all men will believe. – Romans 15:19

- Lord, let me not minister in word only, or human wisdom; rather, cause me to minister in demonstrations of the Holy Spirit and power. Let men's faith be in You, in Your power and in Your presence! – 1 Corinthians 2:4,5; 4:20

- Lord, let the Holy Spirit fill my heart with supernatural love that the world may believe I am Your disciple. Let me minister in love. – Romans 5:5; John 15:9-12

- Now Lord, cover my head for the day of battle. – Psalm 140:7

- Let the angels of the Lord encamp around me and protect me. – Psalm 34:7

- I overcome the devil by the blood of the Lamb, the word of my testimony, and that I do not love my life to the death, for the sake of Christ. – Revelation 12:11

- I sprinkle the blood of Jesus and receive multiplied grace and peace. – 1 Peter 1:1-2

- I release the voice of the blood against demons and evil spirits that would accuse and condemn me. I command them to be silent and depart. – Hebrews 12:24

- I eat and drink the body and blood of Jesus. – John 6:54

- I have protection, provision, and redemption through the blood of Jesus. I plead the blood over my life and ministry, over all I have, because I am redeemed from the power of evil. – Ephesians 1:7

- Lord, release Your fire and burn up the works of darkness around my life and ministry. – Jeremiah 23:29

- Baptize me with the Holy Spirit and fire; let Your fire be in my heart, my hands, my belly, and my mouth. Let me preach with tongues of fire. – Matthew 3:11-12

- Let Your glory kindle a burning like a fire. – Isaiah 10:16

- Let the fire of Your presence be released in this time. – Psalm 97:5

- Lord, release Your thunderbolts, Your lightning, and scatter the enemy in this place. – Psalm 144: 6

- In Jesus' name, I whet my glittering sword and render vengeance against Your enemies. – Deuteronomy 32:41

- Lord, send forth Your arrows and scatter the enemies of the Lord in this place. – Psalm 18:14

- Release the bow of Judah and the arrows of Ephraim. – Zechariah 3:12-14

- Lord, release Your glorious power. – Exodus 15:6

- I bind up all levels and powers of evil over this service; nothing shall interfere with this time. – Mattthew 16:16-18

- Lord, bless and refresh Your people in this place.

- Bless and refresh the ministers and ministries.

- Let Your kingdom come and Your will be fully done in this place.

- Lord of Hosts, send forth all the hosts of heaven, angels and beings, to bring forth Your Word, Your purpose in this place of dominion. – Psalm 103:20-22

- Lord, I am prospering coming into this place, now let me prosper exceedingly going out. – Deuteronomy 28

Randy DeMain may be contacted through his ministry website:
www.kingdomrevelation.org

www.xppublishing.com
A ministry of XP Ministries